The Unofficial Guidebook to
SURVIVING LIFE WITH TODDLERS

Tiffany O'Connor and Lyndee Brown

Copyright © 2019 Hashtaglifewithboys, LLC

All rights reserved.

No Part of this book may be used, reproduced, or transmitted in any matter whatsoever, including but not limited to electronic or mechanical means, photocopying, recording, or by any information storage and retrieval system without written permission in writing from the author, except in the case of brief quotations embodied in critical articles and reviews.

ISBN: 0960091300
ISBN-13: 978-0960091300 (HCCR Books)

THIS BOOK IS DEDICATED TO THE CHILDREN OF EACH AND EVERY WRITER WHO CONTRIBUTED A STORY IN THIS BOOK. WITHOUT ALL OF YOU THIS BOOK WOULD NOT HAVE BEEN POSSIBLE. YOUR PARENTS LOVE YOU VERY MUCH!

CONTENTS

Foreword ix

1. Is That Pee in My Hair?! 1
2. How to Speak Toddler. A Basic Translation Guide. 6
3. Learning to Swim 10
4. Raising Toddlers Can Be Gross 15
5. Fifteen Habits of a Highly Successful Toddler 19
6. The Literal Son 24
7. Are You TRYING To Embarrass Me? 28
8. Mommy's Popsicles 33
9. Public Restrooms: A Very Specific Kind of Torture 37
10. The "Raur Raurs" Are Coming 42
11. Grocery Shopping with Toddlers is SO MUCH FUN! .. 46
12. Are You Smarter Than A Toddler? 50
13. Notes from the Grand Bedtime Experiment 55
14. Wipe My Butt 59
15. Knick-Knock Jokes 64
16. What to Expect After Potty Training 70
17. Burning Questions, Nick. Jr. Edition 74
18. Letter of Final Warning 78
19. Daddy Words 83
20. Toddlers, Hazmat Suits, and the Most Wonderful Time of the Year 87
21. The Terrifying Threes 91
22. If Only Our Mama's Told Us There'd "Pee" Days Like This 95
23. A Day in the Life of a Toddler 99
24. For Whom the Smell Tolls 103
25. Muffin Wars 108

26. Hell Hath No Fury Like A Toddler Who Didn't Get Her
    Pony Toothbrush 113
27. Pint Size Politician 116
28. Mother and Daughter Talks.. 120
29. From Wallflower to Founding Member of The Mall
    Running Club... 125
30. Toddler Battles... 129
31. Is It Poop or Is It Chocolate?.. 133
32. Preschooler Meltdowns 101... 137

About the Authors... 141
Letter from the Editors..149

FOREWORD

BUNMI LADITAN
(Author of *The Honest Toddler* and *Toddlers are A**holes: It's Not Your Fault*)

Being a parent means you've survived the newborn phase and infant phase only to assume you're now out of the woods. In a sense, you are. Instead of being afraid your baby's neck can't support its head, you're afraid of getting slapped by a power-hungry three-year-old who skipped his nap. Instead of being worried your infant will wake up in the night, you know without a doubt that your toddler will. And she'll probably want some midnight cereal. Toddlerhood is when your child becomes part human, part despot, part puppy. There will be hugs, wet kisses, and authority battles. And lots of pee.

Toddlers are human beings are their peak cuteness and this is by no accident. God, in His infinite mercy, knew we would need this adorableness to survived this sleep deprived, kicking off shoes in the car seat, throwing Goldfish crackers in the toilet, refusing to potty train period in our children's lives. And somehow, when it's all over...you'll miss it. Your mind will block out all of the grocery store tantrums, fade them into the background of your memory closet and all you'll remember are chubby arms around your neck and how your child looks like a full-fledged cherub as they speak.

You WILL survive this. One day and one candy bribe at a time.

Love, Bunmi

IS THAT PEE IN MY HAIR?!
K.C. RUNKEL

"Give a toddler a snack, and he'll eat for a day. Teach him to get his own snack, and you'll be digging Cheerios out of your cushions until the end of time." ~The Rustic Hideaway

"So are you excited?" my husband asks as I slide the last package of diapers we will ever need for our son across the self-checkout scanner at Target.

"I guess," I answer quietly, shoving my Red Card into the chip reader. That five percent off has really made a difference over the past two years. Diapers, even the generic brand, have cost us a pretty penny. It will be nice to save some money.

He laughs. "You don't sound too enthusiastic."

Though I roll my eyes playfully, inside I am a nervous wreck. I cannot think of a single milestone I have dreaded more since becoming a mother than potty training. Yet, here I am, one small road trip away from diving "waste"-deep into my own nightmare (pun definitely intended).

The date has been circled on the calendar for months, I have read all of the books, and I have an entire week blocked out of my schedule dedicated to nothing but staying at home watching my kid do his business. The plan is set. As soon as we return from our family vacation next week, I will be in full on potty training mode. After months of prep work, you would think I would feel more excited, but I don't.

Why? Because pee and poop are gross when not contained in a diaper. Because I hate doing laundry, and, perhaps more than anything because I will be teaching my son something that will inevitably take him from baby to full-blown toddler. Sure, my mommy heart is more than ready to say sayonara to the diapers and hello to the big boy undies. It's just that atrocious black hole of time in between that has me shaking in my big girl panties.

Fast forward one week. The big day has finally arrived. I take a few extra seconds to kiss my husband goodbye, throwing in an additional hug just before sending him out the door. Sure, it's not as if I am headed off to war or anything, but I do have the eerie feeling that I am on the frontline of a battlefield and survival is not guaranteed.

I start making a mental checklist of everything I have on hand, knowing at any moment my son will be up, and calling for me to come get him.

Potty chair? Check.
Toilet insert? Check.
Pull-ups for naptime? Check.
Potty books? Check.
Clorox wipes? *gasp* Oh…my…goodness. I forgot the Clorox wipes!

Quickly, I race to the cabinet under the kitchen sink, cursing under my breath as I fumble with the child safety lock. Why do they make those things so hard to open? Oh, right.

Finally, I manage to release the lock and begin tearing out each bottle, scattering them chaotically across the kitchen floor. Windex, Dawn dish soap, Febreeze--nothing of use comes out! My heart sinks just a little.

The Unofficial Guidebook to Surviving Life With Toddlers

You've got this," I remind myself. "You've been covered in your child's pee and poo many times before. This is no different."

But it is different because sometime around age one my sweet little boy went from making cute little baby messes in his diaper to giant, man-sized—well, you know. The thought alone is enough to set off my gag reflexes.

Then I hear it. "Mama!" *gulp* Its go-time.

I walk into my son's room, a wide smile set across my face, praying he can't sense how nervous I am. After all, every potty training book agrees that kids pick up on their parent's stress, and I am not about to derail potty training right out of the gate by showing anything but the utmost enthusiasm.

"Hi sweetheart," I say, picking him up out of his crib. "Today is a special day! Do you know why?"

Admittedly, I am laying the cheese on rather thick. Any other morning it would take six cups of coffee to get me here, but not today. Today I will act as if I am auditioning for a leading role on Yo Gabba Gabba, excitement oozing from my every pore.

"Because today you are a big boy," I exclaim, not waiting for him to answer me. "Today, you are going to start using the potty! Isn't that fun?"

The plan is to have him butt naked all day long, so I sit him on the changing table and begin stripping off his pajamas. I try my absolute hardest not to focus on the fact that this is the last diaper I will ever take off of my baby boy. Oh, how the time has gone by so fast! It seems like just yesterday he was—

What was that? Did he just pee on me? Already?

"Stop, stop, stop!" I scream, rushing him out of the room in search of the nearest potty chair (a whole other level below us). I take the stairs two by two, a stream of urine spurting before me, landing in silent plops on the shaggy carpet below. We don't make it to the potty in time, but I shake it off. Accidents happen.

After a filling breakfast of toast, eggs, and juice, I decide the majority of our day should be spent outside. It's 80°, not a cloud in the sky, nor a breath of wind. Plus, if my son pees in the yard a piece of my soul won't die nearly as quickly as when he pees in the house.

We begin playing with trucks on the back patio. With my iPhone, iPad, and computer all tucked away inside, there is no chance of me being distracted from my son even for a second. He has my full attention, and I have to admit, it is rather nice. I mean, how often do I spend this much uninterrupted time with him one-on-one? I need to look at this experience as a blessing in disguise.

As I stare at my naked toddler playing, his cute little tushie running back and forth as he pushes his dump truck across the concrete, I smile and think about just how big he has gotten. Before long he will be in pre-school, then kindergarten, then going off to high school. Oh, I want to cry, it is just so swe—

He shivers.

"Oh, no! Are you cold sweetheart?" I ask. I guess being naked--even in the summer--can bring on a bit of a chill. I decide to go grab him a light jacket from inside.

"Here you are hon—" but I don't get to finish my sentence. As I step out the back door, my foot catches something slick, causing me to fall backward. Pain radiates from my back, and my head down to my rear is now soaking wet. I want so desperately to believe it is just water, but I know in my heart of hearts that it is not just water.

I was gone for thirty freaking seconds! I want to yell. But I don't...because accidents happen.

Staying outside is turning out to be worse than inside, but, trying to be the optimist, I tell myself that something good did come out of it. I now know that shivers mean PEE IS COMING. And before long I also learn what clenched cheeks mean, though that wasn't a big mystery, to begin with.

By the end of the morning, I try to tally up the number of accidents we had. I lose track somewhere around twenty. As it turns out, kids pee…a lot. Especially when you pump them full of juice.

I feed my son a quick lunch on the potty and take him up to his room to nap. I almost want to cry when I see that package of Pull-ups sitting on his bed because—let's face it—they're diapers (though I will NEVER call them that). He goes down without a fuss, apparently just as exhausted as I am.

I lean my back against his closed bedroom door and gently slide to the floor. I could sleep right here, but I won't because there is something far more appealing than sleep calling my name.

I make my way to the bathroom and turn on my shower to just below scorching levels, allowing the steam to fill up every empty space around me. Right now, I need this more than anything. My soul needs rest. My aching muscles need heat.

And there is pee in my hair.

HOW TO SPEAK TODDLER. A BASIC TRANSLATION GUIDE.

JESICA RYZNSKI

"Want to lose any ounce of sanity you may have left? Try setting anything up using a voice-activated system with a toddler and a preschooler in the same room…" ~Is That Chocolate or Poop

Toddlers are pretty amazing little people, because they are in fact, little people. All of a sudden they are no longer squishy little babies who are content to simply sit or lay down all day while you put them wherever you want to put them or take them wherever you decide to go. Suddenly, they have their own ideas about what they want and when they want it, and they are incredibly dedicated to their own little whims. If you have ever had the opportunity to care for a toddler you will know that this is putting it extremely mildly. A toddler who wants something that you either don't understand, or are not able to provide is very much like a tornado, and you my friend are a trailer park.

Heading into the land of toddler myself for the fourth time, I thought that a translation guide of sorts might be helpful. So here we go:

1.) "NO!" OR "I NOT!"

Remember in College when you were insanely dedicated to a cause and decided that you would join your fellow protesters in a sit-in? Nothing, and I mean NOTHING was going to deter you from making sure your message was heard and that change was implemented. This is now your toddler. If you plan on accomplishing anything on the day that these words are uttered, clear your schedule and make some calls, because you are not going anywhere anytime soon.

These words are usually used when it is time to leave the house and socks, shoes, or possibly pants are required. These words are also very popular when trying to buckle a toddler into a car seat when they will suddenly decide to "plank" and use their superhuman toddler strength to prevent you from doing up the buckle. These words are almost always used when you have to get to work, or you have an appointment which you are likely already running late for.

2.) "I TRY IT."

These words will be used during mealtimes. They mean that your toddler is now going to abandon their own plate, which contains the exact same food that you are desperately trying to eat yourself, and will now proceed to eat every scrap of food on your plate. For some reason, toddler logic dictates that your food is better than theirs, even though it is EXACTLY THE SAME. It's best to just develop a taste for cold, tiny bites of food because unless you hide in the kitchen to eat, you may be trading plates for a while.

3.) "I NO DID IT."

These words will often be uttered when you have been out of the room for a few minutes. It absolutely means that they did something....the trick is what is it? Sometimes it will be obvious because there will be a puddle of something or the writing will literally be on the wall. However, if it is not obvious, do not assume that nothing has happened. Search high and low until you figure it out because this is one of those times when weeks from now you will be wondering what on earth that smell is, only to discover half a banana crammed into the back of the toy garbage truck....

4.) "NO WORRY MOMMY. I CLEAN IT."

These words are also almost always used when you have been out if the room. This one is a bit more alarming. It's nice that they have taken ownership over whatever havoc they have caused, however they have also attempted to clean it up. So, what was the mess? And what exactly did they "clean" it up with? This often involves a defective sippy cup and a throw cushion from your couch. Or, worst case scenario, a diaper and an afghan…probably knitted by great grandma and irreplaceable.

5.) "I BIG HELPER."

This is a tough one because it is so darn cute, but it's a trick. Do not be fooled by the big innocent eyes or angelic smile. This does not mean they are going to help you. This statement means they are going to, under the guise of helping you, do absolutely everything in their power to prevent you from getting the activity done. If you give in to this request, as I foolishly do at least once a day, pour yourself a coffee and just abandon all hope of getting anything accomplished. Oh, and make sure you allow for time to clean up whatever messes will now be caused by your "big helper."

6.) "I HUNGRY."

Brace yourself. You are about to be told "No" to every single option of nourishment that you provide and even though the toddler could actually be hungry, there will not be a single food item in this world that will be acceptable. If there are older children in the home, your toddler will also be aware that you have cookies. You know that sit-in from College? You are about to meet the "sit-in" King or Queen.

7.) "MINE."

Toddlers are only capable of understanding their own needs. So this statement could refer to a toy, a toilet brush or even your left shoe. It doesn't have to make sense. In fact, it often doesn't. Just assume that everything they see, touch, hear or smell belongs to them in their little world and roll with it.

8.) "IT SO PRETTY."

This rarely means that you will find whatever is happening "pretty". It could mean that those paints and crayons you thought you had hidden have been located and in the time it took you to pee, your little artist has provided you with a custom made mural in your living room. This mural will likely include walls and your couch. It could mean that somehow your toddler has found a pair of scissors (even safety ones will cut hair) and given themselves a "pretty" new haircut. Or, it could refer to the fact that your toddler located a tube of lipstick in your purse and has given themselves a "pretty" new makeover. It could also refer to the fact that you have thirty seconds to get out the door for an appointment and your toddler has removed every scrap of clothing you put on them and opted for a diaper and a tutu, a pair of your underwear on their head and one glove instead….they may combine this with the lipstick makeover.

9.) "I WUV YOU."

No translation required here. Once these words are spoken, usually by a sleepy toddler after the tenth story and following a day filled with the contents of this list, you will melt. Nothing that happened that day will matter in the slightest. At that moment you will be filled with joy in the knowledge that this stubborn, messy and infuriating little person is your little person. Your amazing little person who is growing up before your eyes and finding their own unique ways to explore the world every day. And that is amazing. Also, toddlers are still pretty squishy.

LEARNING TO SWIM
JENNIFER LIZZA

"As mothers, we don't expect our children to be perfect. We need to allow ourselves the same expectations. Motherhood is messy. Embrace the mess." ~Outsmarted Mommy

First comes pregnancy, then comes the baby stage, and before you know it you haven't slept in years and you have this human being with endless energy and a shocking amount of willpower. They refer to them as toddlers, and yes this stage seems to arrive at warp speed. It could be that the newborn stage and baby stage fly by like a blur because like I said, you're tired. It could also be that you put your adorable baby to bed one night and they woke up a toddler with little to no warning.

When you are a parent you realize rather quickly that having little to no warning about what lies around the corner of each stage is pretty much par for the course. The most ironic part of the changes and stages is that once you finally have a stage mastered, or at the very least you figure out how to feed them, they go and change.

Admittedly, I was never a huge fan of the newborn stage. I felt like it was a bucket of pressure-induced stress to have this little human depending on me for their survival. They can't even hold up their head let alone tell you why they are crying for eight straight hours. The sleep deprivation during this stage is something out of a Stephen King novel; no I'm not being dramatic. I'm being honest. My favorite stage was when my boys turned six months. This stage was bliss. They were finally sleeping. They had little personalities and would laugh at all of my jokes. That's right. I finally had an audience who thought I was the funniest person on the planet. Talk about an ego boost.

By eight months they were starting to eat food that no longer resembled dog poop. It was a real step forward. Little words were being uttered and I felt like I was getting to know the little humans we created. I truly loved this stage. The moment they said mama and dada my heart grew a little. When they started blowing kisses and hugging with all their might my heart grew a lot. This was the motherhood I had read about. This was amazing.

One night I put my oldest son to bed. I kissed his forehead and told him I loved him; he looked at me and said "wuv mama." I closed his door and let out a blissful sigh. Little did I know there was a change in the air. There was no warning. No one told me how fast it happens or early signs to look out for so I could be prepared. I know now that other parents can't warn you about these things, because they too are just trying to keep their ship afloat and navigate the new waters without a life jacket. Parents nod at one another as our ships pass. We understand with just a look that we are not alone. We understand that we are not the only ones trying to figure out what on earth we are doing on a regular basis.

If you need proof of this head to a Target during the day. Peruse the aisles. Follow the sounds of the whining. Follow the signs of the pleas and demands to sit down because shopping carts are not for toddler surfing. Look at the faces of the parents you pass and take note at the nods and looks that tell you this is parenting a toddler. Try not to get scared, because there's really no avoiding it. There will be a short period of time that will feel longer than any other period of time that has come before it. You will sweat. You will cry, and you will most certainly argue about ridiculous topics with a smaller version of yourself.

I'm happy to tell you, however, that you will survive. You really will. I know, because I survived two toddlers and am here to tell you I survived, I'm also a really good wrestler now so that's a plus.

Toddlers are like your drunken college roommate. You have no idea what is going to set them off. You know that you need to tell them no more juice, but you also know that this will cause a fight. You watch them like a hawk because you know they are a flight risk and as they start to get tired you hope and pray they will stay awake until you get home because once they wake up they will just want to eat and run around while crying. It's a lot of pressure to be in charge of a toddler.

My son was always up for an outing. I loved our little trips to the grocery store, the library, and the bagel shop. It was a Tuesday, and I told my mom I would pick her up so we could do a little shopping and go to lunch. I didn't know at the time that my son had literally changed in his sleep. We shopped without issue and decided to go to a bagel shop for a light lunch. He happily sat in his high chair eating his bagel and waiving at all the old people who thought he was the cutest. I happened to agree with all of them. As we were leaving he decided he didn't want to hold my hand.

"Buddy you have to hold mommy's hand. We are going into a parking lot."

"NO!"

Nervously laughing. "Bud mommy is not kidding. You have to hold my hand ok?"

"NO! NO!! NO!!!" At this point, he threw himself on the floor of the bagel shop. I stood there partly wondering what the hell was happening to my child and partly thinking about all the gross germs he was proceeding to roll around in. I decided I was going to just pick him up. Mind you I was six months pregnant with my youngest at the time, but so what. He was two years old, how difficult could this be?

Well, my son had superhuman strength and speed. Before I knew it he ran out the door and took off down the shopping mall's sidewalk. I felt one million eyes on me as I chased my two-year-old begging him to stop. He laughed and laughed and ran faster and faster. I finally caught up to him just before he was about to run into the parking lot. I pulled him by the hood of his coat, thankful that it was still ridiculously cold in April here in New Jersey.

As I tried to catch my breath thinking this was a close call, and thankful it was over, my son proceeded to lie on the ground and throw an epic fit. He was kicking and screaming and impossible to get up. All I could think was what on earth did I feed this kid yesterday? Oh crap, maybe he's allergic to bagels. That must be it. This is some weird reaction to the dough from the bagel. It has to be. As I made a mental note to call the allergist as soon as possible my son calmed down enough for me to pick him up and head to the car.

When we got to the car he made his body stiff as an ironing board making it impossible to strap him into his car seat. I put him in the backseat and my mom and I got into the front. We sat in the car listening to my child scream, cry, and kick the seat for what felt like two days. I was going to call my husband to bring us food and water when I realized it had only been three minutes. THREE MINUTES. It felt like forever. I hadn't watched time pass this slowly since that philosophy class in college. I don't remember sweating like this though in that class. Nope, I definitely didn't sweat like this.

After three minutes passed the car was suddenly silent. I turned around and my son was sound asleep. I got out and strapped him into his car seat. My mom looked at me with a look that said, we survived. I proceeded to call my pediatrician's office, because...first-time mom syndrome. I explained what had happened and asked if I should bring him in.

"Mrs. Lizza (hiding her laughter, not well I might add) I'm sorry to tell you but you officially have a toddler. This will not be the last time this happens. They are strong-willed and love to test the waters. You will learn to swim better with time. Hang in there."

That's it? That was her advice? I thought I already swam pretty well thank you very much. I got home and my husband asked how our day was.

"Not great. You and I are going to have to take swimming lessons."

"What? Why? Are we entering a swim race I don't know about?"

"Yup. It's called toddlerhood and the water is rough. It's really rough."

As time passed we both learned how to navigate the waters of toddlerhood. We didn't always do it perfectly, but we learned more as we swam along. We survived that stage with a few bruises along the way, but we did it.

Our boys are ten and seven now. We just recently entered the eye roll stage so I signed us up for swim lessons in the preteen pool. This one might require a life jacket. I'm going to keep swimming through until I am able to lie on the beach one day and watch my boys swim all on their own. That may wind up being the hardest stage of all.

RAISING TODDLERS CAN BE GROSS
CASSIE HILT

"Parenthood is having to apologize to your toddler because you told them it was sunny out and they wanted to tell you." ~The Chronicles of Motherhood

Toddlers are interesting creatures. They are these tiny balls of endless energy, bouncing and shrieking all day long. They have no concept of time or schedules. For example, if they wake up at three in the morning, they are ready to start their day. There's no convincing them that another four hours of sleep will benefit them, or that it's not time to play yet. You can't reason with a toddler, it's like trying to have a conversation with a honey badger. It just isn't going to happen.

Living with toddlers is a major adjustment in itself. It's sort of like living with a friend whose drunk all the time. They're constantly slurring their words, stumbling all over the place, and telling you the same story over and over again. Clearly, they could use your help with the simple everyday tasks, but when you offer, they refuse, insistent that they can do it themselves.

Toddlers are also masters at creating messes. Did you know it only takes the average toddler .02 seconds to destroy a room? I mean, that's just based off my own research, but I think it's like 99.9% accurate. If you have a toddler at home, chances are it looks like a tiny tornado has gone through your house at any given moment. Others may try, but toddlers are quite skilled in making horrendous messes.

Toddlers can also be gross. Like, really, really gross.

When my oldest son was about two years old, he had started the disgusting habit of randomly reaching into his diaper. I had heard other parents talk about how their kids had done this before. Of course, I was appalled and assumed that my child would never do something so repulsive. At this point in time, he had done this on a few separate occasions. I had either discovered it on our furniture or noticed it on his tiny little fingers (insert gagging noise here).

Well, one day I was getting ready to go run some errands when all of a sudden I heard a high pitched, death scream. Fellow mamas know the scream I'm talking about. The one where it makes your heart drop into your stomach and causes you to simultaneously pee your pants at the same time.

Of course, I instantly panicked and ran into my son's room. He was behind his bedroom door, and his little fingers were pinched near the hinges. I quickly scooped him up and began consoling him, his chubby little face buried in my chest, his arms, wrapped around my neck. It took me a few minutes to calm him down, but of course, mama's hugs always make things better, don't they?

After a few minutes had passed, I put him down and began to clean up his room.

I started to pick up some toys, and as he was 'helping' me, that familiar smell wafted through the air. "Oh man buddy, you need a diaper change", I said.

I quickly got him cleaned out of his messy diaper and picked up where I had left off with cleaning his room.

But I could still smell that dirty diaper…..but I guess, I mean, sometimes that happens, right? Sometimes that stench just lingers in the room, like that second cousin who overstays their welcome and doesn't know when to leave. So I just shrugged it off and kept cleaning.

Once I got to the toy box, I noticed some brown smudges on it…..what in the world…..I was pretty sure I knew what it was. I mean, I definitely wasn't dumb enough to smell it, but it looked fresh and I assumed that since I had just changed him, chances are it wasn't chocolate. My little poop ninja must have reached into his diaper and done it again! After cleaning up the toy box, I quickly grabbed the boy and headed to the bathroom where we washed his hands a few times, just to make sure he was nice and clean.

I headed back into the kitchen to start lunch. There was that smell again…..I checked his diaper just in case he had re-charged already. Nope, clean. Maybe when he reached into the diaper, he had got it on his clothes too? So I proceeded to change his outfit.

WHAT THE HELL! It still smells like CRAP! Was that diaper so powerful that it was stuck in my nostril hairs? It didn't seem like that bad of a poop. I mean, it definitely wasn't as bad as the time he ate those onion rings at the drive-thru (side note: that diaper was so bad, I have never eaten onion rings from that particular fast food chain again, as it takes me back to that awful diaper change of 2011 *shudders*).

I walked around the house, searching for more poop smudges, but I couldn't find anything. Not a poop fingerprint in sight. Nothing. But that smell. IT WOULD NOT GO AWAY! I mean, if you've never scoured your house to try and figure out where a foul smell is coming from, are you even a mom?

Finally about an hour later I remembered that I needed to go to the store. It was getting late and despite the fact that I was semi-ready, I really didn't feel like finishing up my makeup and hair. I decided I would just quickly use the bathroom, and I'd be on my way.

As I was washing my hands afterward, I quickly glanced up in the mirror. And that's when I saw it. The brown smudges. It was peanut butter, I immediately thought. I did have a PB sandwich earlier, although I didn't remember eating it so aggressively that it would be on my face and neck.

Was it from the boy? Maybe he had gotten it on me? I went to wipe the smudges off with my hands, and that's when I realized that it was not, in fact, peanut butter.

There was actual SHIT on my face and neck.

Here I had spent the last two hours trying to figure out where that damn smell was coming from, and it was on me the entire time.

I came to the conclusion that the poop ninja was digging in his diaper right before he got his little fingers stuck in the door. When I went to go comfort him, he had wrapped his poop hands around my neck, smearing it all over me.

I'd love to tell you that this was the only time I have ever found someone else's poop on me, but I think we both know I'd be lying. Three kids later and somehow I still manage to randomly find fecal matter on me. I know they always say to cherish every moment--- that it goes by so quickly. But seriously people, I will not miss finding brown streaks on my clothes.

The 'old me' freaked out when I noticed poop on my neck. But the current me? The more seasoned and experienced, mom of three? It takes more than a little excrement to freak me out these days.

So, some of my best advice to new moms: "Don't sweat the shit stains."

FIFTEEN HABITS OF A HIGHLY SUCCESSFUL TODDLER

KAREN LESH

"80% of parenting is wondering why your sock is wet." ~M.O.B. Truths

A baby can dictate how a household works – when you eat, when you sleep, when you can sit down, whether or not you'll get your errands done, whether you can manage to shower or eat breakfast, and pretty much everything else. A toddler is also quite powerful, but with a twist that keeps you on your toes and always learning more and more about what it means to be a parent. Whether you have one child, or if the toddler is a newly minted "big sibling," they are savvy and successful in testing your limits in patience, thinking on your feet, and simultaneously loving and wanting to scream.

How do these little guys do it? The most successful toddlers have been known to engage in the following key habits, turning you into a weary but well-seasoned parent:

1. Requesting specific food and refusing it. This is the miraculous skill of insisting they're not hungry, then instantaneously being famished and demanding, for example, a waffle. Not a square waffle, but a round waffle. Not with syrup, but with butter and chocolate chips. Not at the table, but at the counter. Not with milk, but with water. And, once you've got the order straight, they dismiss the delectable breakfast and say they will only eat cereal instead. And they mean it!

Impact on the parent: YOU eat the waffle in front of the child, reestablishing your authority, part disgruntled and part excited about your sweet breakfast. Of course while getting the toddler a bowl of cereal.

2. Requiring a specific color sippy cup. The key to this is that the toddler strictly enforces the policy that absolutely no sippy cup other than the one that is unavailable at the time will be acceptable. Orange? NOPE. The toddler wants yellow. Red with yellow polka dots? Again, NO.

Impact on the parent: This is a sanity test. It is possible that the child changes their mind about which color they want along the way, making you question the several minutes you've spent trying to get them to drink out of the cup you have. But no matter what, the one they want is unavailable.

3. Forcing you to fill the kiddie pool. And then simply never, ever, EVER going in it.

Impact on the parent: Annoyance that you inflated the darn thing and spent the time watching it fill up, and more frustration that you don't get to sit by it and dip your feet in for a moment of relaxation.

4. Throwing a tantrum in public. I remember judging parents before I was a parent. We all did that, right? If I saw a mom yelling at her kid, I assumed she was a mean mom who had no control. But when my oldest son, in his time as a feisty toddler, actually sprawled out on the grocery store floor kicking and pounding his fists because he wanted a cupcake, I walked a mile, or at least two grocery store aisles, in all those out-of-control moms' shoes. I responded calmly but firmly many times and ultimately ended up taking his arm and dragging him a few feet (I couldn't lift him because I was mega-pregnant with baby number two and was carrying many groceries . . . not my finest logistical day), causing a scene, and certainly being judged by anyone who did not have kids.

Impact on the parent: This is a resilience test. Will you give in to avoid being judged in public? Or hold strong and find a way out of this? Stay strong, comrades!

5. Refusing story time all day and insisting on "one more" story (six times over) at bedtime. This strategy is most effective when you are stressed out about balancing parenting and life and doing everything as well as you can – for example when you have a presentation to write for work that night, and you haven't slept in years.

Impact on the parent: This is a multifaceted test, requiring you to display excellence in negotiating, prioritizing, and managing stress. My route out of this is typically to negotiate one story, give in and read two, then shuffle away with a hug and a kiss knowing I spent quality time with my toddler before doing the other things I have to get done.

6. Peeing or pooping in their pants shortly after being potty-trained. This strategic move typically happens the only time you forget to pack a change of clothes.

Impact on the parent: This is the panic test. Will you stop what you're doing and head home for a change of clothes? Or hope nobody smells or sees and you just carry-on, wiping the look of surprise off your face? (Note: I've done both)

7. Licking things. Whether it's bath toys or the shower door or – GASP! – the handle of the shopping cart, it's cringe-worthy.

Impact on the parent: I think of this as the "varied response" test. "Yuck that's germy!" usually results in the kid licking the thing again. "That's disgusting; please stop." – Same result. Freaking out and trying to instantly sanitize the surface and, somehow, the kid's mouth – triggers laughter and joy...and then licking again. The best response here takes a lot of self-control for the parent: Take a deep breath, think about germ exposure bolstering the immune system, and don't over-react. (Easier said than done!)

8. Swearing. Like the time my middle son came out of the bathroom and told me, "F*&# is what you say when all the paper cups fall into the toilet. Well, that's when Daddy said it." Noting the smirk on my face, he continued to say the f-word... undoubtedly at daycare that day, too.

Impact on the parent: Swears flying out of a toddler's mouth can be hilarious, but also embarrassing. Alternatively, they seem to bond caregivers in a collective "oops" noting that we all slip up and swear now and then (read: often). And it's up to our toddlers to "out" us.

9. "No." Aside from swears, the savvy toddler knows how to frequently respond with "No!" even when it wouldn't be so objectionable to say "yes." Putting on shoes? "No!" How about painting a picture? "No!!" More chicken for dinner? "No!!!"

Impact on the parent: This is the frustration test. It builds tolerance so you can carry on with your day with some assurance of knowing you can at least predict what your toddler's response to a given situation will be.

10. Independence. This often manifests itself in activities like insisting on opening their own single-serve applesauce or yogurt. We know how this ends. SPLAT.

Impact on the parent: This is merely a skill test – how quickly can you wipe up the mess, either with a spoon or a wet paper towel.

11. Letting go . . . of the helium balloon they bawled their eyes out for at the parade, and then sobbing as they watch it soar its way up to the clouds.

Impact on the parent: Utter sorrow, as you remember this happening to you as a kid. So, you go buy another balloon.

12. Taking a long, long, long (did I mention long?) time. The same toddler who can run naked through the living room lightning fast can and will take a ridiculously long time to do just about anything you need them to do quickly. Inevitably, on the days you have to make it out of the house early, the toddler will want a second breakfast, or will want to pretend to tie their shoes, or zip their jacket, each of which can take fifteen minutes or more.

Impact on the parent: This is the ultimate test of patience. No matter how much planning ahead you do – allowing extra time to get these things done – it won't happen. Encouraging faster movement seems to slow the activities down to slow motion. You just have to deal with it, and remind yourself to cherish every moment of these adorable early years.

13. Making messes. Crumpling paper, coloring with markers on the table, covering themselves in finger paint from their fingers to the top of their head, dumping out a bowl of soup and mushy noodles, even smearing poop on the wall. Toddlers are the masters of mess.

Impact on the parent: A tolerance test. Another case for a deep breath, and a chance to enjoy the chaos of childhood.

14. Sleeping in your bed. Many toddlers are expert at wiggling their way into your bed by ensuring that everyone gets back to sleep more quickly in that situation than with you standing in their bedroom door telling them over and over to get back into their own bed.

Impact on the parent: Snuggle up. Habits 1 through 13 can wear you down. Let this one melt you. They won't be in your bed forever.

15. Smiling. Toddlers still have those baby cheeks and soft skin, and often not quite a full mouth of teeth yet. When they smile, we see a glimpse back to the days when we were first getting to know them. The days we never will forget.

Impact on the parent: We melt again. We smile back. And the toddler gets their way.

Here's to raising successful humans, from toddlerhood to beyond, and becoming good, seasoned parents as we go.

THE LITERAL SON
KARSSON HEVIA

"Toddlers are more akin to unicorns than humans. Why? Because they're a TODDLER!" ~2manyopentabs

From day one, my oldest son has always been a very serious guy. He's determined and steadfast, committed and judicious about everything he puts his mind to. Whether it be constructing an intricate series of Lego cities or scooting with friends in the neighborhood, drawing detailed submarines, or solving math problems; it's always met with a steady level of intensity. And don't get me wrong, he has lots of fun doing all of those things, but make no mistake about it, it's serious business. There's never a light-heartedness or penchant towards the easy-going. He's my sweet-as-sugar, tell-it-like-it-is, always literal kid.

This tendency towards the literalness and taking everything at face value (typically coupled with a heavy sprinkling of stubbornness), has provided a fair share of humorous occasions over the years, starting at a very young age.

Take, for instance, Hudson's 1st birthday party. We'd invited all our friends and family to celebrate in the special day with us. It was to be a day of memories made, happiness had, and a milestone remembered. After playing with friends and opening several presents, it was time for CAKE.

Now, given that as a whole, we typically eat very clean, limiting sugar and sweets, I figured that the fact that Hudson had never seen a cake in person, nor ever tasted one, he would want to jump right in and devour the giant birthday delicacy we'd set before him. However, even at the ripe age of just one, there was no way this kid was smashing anything all over himself. Somehow, he just knew far too well that rubbing cake on his face would be a ridiculous notion. One that would make you look like an absolute idiot (after all, a cake was for eating, not smashing), so he opted for eating some later (like when everyone wasn't staring at him, and he could eat in a civilized manner). Ehh, Animals.

Fast-forward to age two. Hudson was an incredibly verbal and literate kid very early on, so by this age, he'd already mastered the alphabet as well as the correct sequence of letters. One day while playing with his magnetic letters on his chalkboard, he asked me one afternoon where the 'other N' was. I had assumed he'd misplaced the match to either the upper or lower case consonant. No. Not the case. He had both right in front of him, in perfect order, after 'M' and before 'O.' He wanted the other 'N.' Hmmm. Right. So, I started by telling him that there, in fact, was only one 'N' and explained the rationale behind why.

This was not satisfactory. He was convinced beyond a shadow of a doubt that it had gone missing, and was prepared to just wait it out until it had been recovered. We continued this back-and-forth for a few days until he either came to his senses, realizing that 'N' was the one and only, or came to the foregone conclusion that his mother was an idiot who clearly, hadn't mastered the alphabet yet, and to stop asking. I'm still not sure which.

As Hudson grew from young toddler to an older, more advanced version, so too did his instances of literalness. This story has since taken the cake.

On the way to basketball one foggy early evening, my son turned to his friend in the car (with whom was carpooling with us to practice) and asked if he could see that sketch drawn on the inside of the passenger window.

Rewind to that prior weekend, my husband, myself, and our two boys, Hudson and Hawkins, were heading into Sausalito for a fun morning hike to see a lighthouse. It was a very foggy start to the morning while driving there, and for whatever adolescent-fueled reason, my husband had the impulse to draw a penis on the inside of the window and laugh about it with the two boys in the backseat. Now, this eludes me on many levels, but mainly because I lack a penis and so talking about penises, drawing penises, or even thinking much about penises other than where they're peeing with them, pretty much doesn't occupy my thought processes.

So, after the raucous of erupting laughter subsided, I immediately make my husband erase the fine work of art, to which he immediately responded by drawing a heart. Fine. I'll take it.

Now, back to the drive to basketball.

Does anyone remember what happens to windows when they fog up? You. See. Everything. That. Was. Once. On. Them.

So yes, Hudson proceeds to tell his friend that his Daddy drew a penis on the window. And since the friend was a dude, he also thought the story hilarious. But it doesn't stop there; my literal child makes the story so much more cringe worthy. He then finishes the story by telling him that Daddy drew a heart next to the penis- but that he wasn't sure why, but that he thinks it's maybe because mommy likes big penises….

I'm just going to let that hang there for a moment on the page.

Yes, because MOMMY LIKES BIG PENISES...

I never knew I could be so mortified in front of a five-year-old in my life. I literally burst out every excuse as to why that statement that my child had just belted out was, in fact, false, yet all seemed to make the situation ten times worse.

This is how it sounded; 'no, I don't like big penises, I mean, not like I like little ones, I don't like penises! Well, not like AT ALL, just not right now. Not in the way that you think I'm saying it. This is not going well. Let's please not mention this conversation happened, OK? In fact, let's discuss something else altogether. Like the weather… no, not the weather (that's what got us here in the first place)! I'm going to KILL YOUR FATHER!

Having a literal kid has taught me time and again, that it doesn't mean they're short on imagination or stunted by a lack of wonderment associated with being a child. Conversely, for us, it actually just means that Hudson has always been incredibly grounded. He asks questions when things don't add up (hello, Easter Bunny), he gives pause to answers that he doesn't understand the answer to (because I said so), and pursues the rationale behind them. But the one thing I can attest to is that having a child who takes all things at a literal level, brings lots of laughs to a family, shedding light on just how ridiculous life (and the moments within it) can be.

I wouldn't change my little man for the world and having had his beautiful take on the world, has enlightened me in more ways than I could have ever imagined a now six-year-old could have. He'll make big waves someday, I just know it.

ARE YOU TRYING TO EMBARRASS ME?
SANDRA SAMOSKA

"My toddler: "I do it myself."
AKA
We will now be late for everything
FOREVER!" ~Outnumbered

I am convinced that one of the driving forces in the life of a toddler is to creatively and repeatedly embarrass his or her parents. I don't just mean the fairly common embarrassing moments – potty accidents, screaming tantrums in the grocery store, or repeating to Grandma that bad word you let slip the other day when the driver in front of you slammed on his brakes.

No, I mean sink-into-the-ground, pretend-you're-invisible, I-can-never-show-my-face-here-again embarrassments. The ones that leave you standing there frozen in mortification, wishing actively for a giant meteor to fall from the sky and land on your head.

When my daughter was a two-year-old, she loved a show on PBS called Wild Kratts. It came on some time after Sesame Street but before BBC World News America. It was about two brothers who could wear special suits that allowed them to change into different animals, and they went on adventures where they could use unique creature powers to rescue different species from the dastardly humans who wanted to exploit them. It was pretty cute, and my daughter learned a lot of fun facts about animals around the world. Nothing wrong with that, right?

One lovely Sunday, I walked down the children's wing to pick my daughter up from her Sunday school classroom after service. Her teacher greeted me at the door and said, "We need to talk."

"Oh. Ok. Is something wrong?"

"Yes," she said with a frown. "While we were talking about Noah's Ark, your daughter told the class that she likes to watch the Crack Brothers with their Power Dicks."

I actually felt my entire body turn red and then fade to pale white. My first response was horrified laughter, but after looking at the teacher's face, I could tell that wouldn't be welcome.

She went on. "At first I was sure I misheard. 'Power what?' Then another little boy chimed in, 'Dicks. Dicks. You know, DICKS.'"

I tried to explain that they were the Kratt Brothers, and they used Power Discs.

She didn't believe me.

I really miss that church.

A few years later, my daughter's younger sister came along. After being accused of letting my oldest watch porn by the Sunday school teacher, I figured nothing much else would embarrass me.

How wrong I was.

One memorable summer vacation, our family, along with my husband's sisters and their families, and my mother- and father-in-law went out to dinner. By this time my oldest was four, and my youngest was about two. Bringing a large group to a restaurant in a tourist town in the middle of the peak season made the wait for our table over an hour. An hour is a pretty long time for an adult, but it is a lifetime for two young children.

By the time we got our table and placed our drink orders, my daughters had reached their limit for good behavior. Patience had flown out the window long before, especially for my littlest, who informed me in her most demanding voice that she was starving. We'd already mowed through the complimentary crackers on the table, and we still had a while before we could expect the food to arrive.

I tried to distract her.

"Would you like to color?" NO!

"Want to sit with Mimi?" NO!!

"What would you like?" FOOD!!!

Because I was pretty hungry by that point and I didn't relish being thrown out of the restaurant before our food arrived, in desperation, I handed my toddler the garnish from my drink. She seemed pretty happy with her orange slice and calmed down for the next few minutes while we waited.

Soon the food arrived, and we all started in on our long-awaited meal. After a few bites, I looked over and saw my daughter swaying in her seat. Her eyelashes were fluttering, and her head started doing that jerky, I'm-about-to-pass-out bob on her neck. I had one moment to look in panic at my husband before I shot my hand out and caught my two-year old's face before it landed in her plate of chicken nuggets.

Oh. My. Goodness. I just got my toddler drunk. Please tell me no one noticed. I looked at my husband, and he looked at me. Our eyes shot to the head of the table where my mother-in-law was having a conversation with her daughter.

"We will never speak of this again."

Fast forward a number of years, and my husband and I had four kids. In a moment of madness, we decided it would be a great idea to take the children out to dinner one evening. Our oldest girls, now ten and almost eight, were well behaved. They knew how to use inside voices and behave properly in public.

However, our youngest two, ages four and one, were still in that toddler and pre-school stage of unpredictable, mortifying craziness.

As we walked in the door of a local restaurant, we were happy to see that there would be no wait and they could even fit us in one of their large round booths. This seemed ideal since that way we could scoot the kiddos in the middle, bookending them with a parent on each end. Our toddler's highchair was perfectly placed at the end of the table. That was where our good luck ended.

After the waiter took our drink orders and dropped off the chips and salsa, the fun began. It started when our toddler started banging on the table for chips. While my husband and I were distracted trying to get him to stop banging and simultaneously break a couple of chips up for him, the four-year-old reached across the table and scooped up a huge chip full of spicy salsa. Three seconds later her face turned red, she started coughing uncontrollably and was waving her hands in the air while gasping, "Water! Water!" My husband jumped up to get the bartender to pour us some water while I rubbed her back. That's when the toddler decided to grab his father's fork and knife and use them to bang the table since his hands weren't getting enough attention.

My husband came back with the water, and we got my daughter calmed down and the knife out of my son's hands. At that moment the four-year-old popped up on her knees to reach for more chips and knocked the glass of ice water the bartender had given us all over the table. And her lap. And my purse. And her sister. This was followed by her saying, in her loudest voice for all to hear, "MY BOOTY IS COLD!"

Once that was clean – the water on the table, not her wet booty – the waiter brought our queso. Oh good, I thought, something for the baby to eat, so he would stop trying to stab me in the hand with the fork he somehow kept getting ahold of.

That's when our preschooler announced loudly, "I HAVE TO GO POTTY." As I was getting up to let her out of the booth so that my husband could take her to the restroom, the toddler decided he'd had enough of waiting and maneuvered out of his high chair, onto the table, and started CRAWLING ACROSS THE TABLE to the chip bowl.

That was the first ten minutes of our dinner out. We hadn't even ordered yet. I'm pretty sure by this time the restaurant employees had put our table on red alert status and had all been warned to do everything in their power to get us out of there as quickly and quietly as possible.

By the end of dinner, my husband and I had said, "I'm so sorry," no less than eight times to various diners, wait staff, and even a memorable conversation with the restaurant manager. The next time we went to that restaurant we vowed to leave our kids at home and wear disguises – just in case they added us to a watch list.

I'm not sure why toddlers are programmed to embarrass their parents, but I do know that the only reason we put up with it (and in my case do it over and over) is because they can just be so darn cute. I think it's a conspiracy.

MOMMY'S POPSICLES
LAUREN EBERSPACHER

"TODDLER SCREAMING BLOODY MURDER!!!

Me racing down the hallway thinking his leg is broken, the bones are sticking out of his skin, there's going to be blood everywhere…

Toddler is sitting in the middle of the room and can't pull off his sock." ~From Blacktop to Dirt Road

My oldest daughter is definitely the most inquisitive of my three kids. She is always asking what, why, and how about everything. And that includes everything that I put in my shopping cart at the store.

Every time "that time of the month" rolled around, I hit the grocery store for my box of "Mommy things," and every time my daughter asked what the blue boxes I put in the cart were for. "Oh honey, those are just special things for mommies. Someday we will talk about it." But once we got home, she would see me put the box under my bathroom vanity, closing the doors and hiding "Mommy's special boxes" behind them. She knew it was a sacred space behind those vanity doors; she just never knew what I was really keeping in there.

A couple of summers ago, we were getting ready to host a new Bible study with some couples in our town. We knew one of the couples pretty well, but most of them were acquaintances, so I had spent a few days getting the house ready before the group came over.

As the evening of the Bible study finally arrived, I naturally had been running around the house getting things picked up, wiping down the counters, and shoving toys back into their bins, so I had very little time to get ready. I was rushing back into my closet when I felt it. "Oh crap, really?" I had started my period, five minutes before our company was supposed to arrive, and I needed to act fast.

I quickly ran over to my vanity and opened the doors to pull out my box of tampons. I opened the box and pulled one out and made my way to the bathroom.

Thinking I was alone, I didn't even close the door behind me. I pulled down my pants, did my business, unwrapped the tampon from its wrapper, stuck it in, and pulled my pants back up. When I turned around from flushing the toilet, I gasped in surprise seeing my daughter standing there watching me, eyes wide open.

"Oh gosh, honey, you scared me! Mommy was just going potty." She didn't move from her spot in front of the bathroom. She just stood there staring at me. "How long have you been standing there for?" I asked her, as I grabbed my tampon wrapper and applicator and threw them in the trash.

"Well, I came in to see what you were doing. And now I finally know what's in those blue boxes you keep secret under the sink."

Oh my gosh, she just watched me put my tampon in. It looks like we are going to have to have "the woman talk" a lot sooner than what I thought we were going to.

"Well yeah honey, you might have some questions now about that. But you know what, our friends are getting ready to come over in just a few minutes. How about we talk about this later tonight after everyone leaves?"

"OK sounds good. But now I know why you hide them. I would do that, too," she said as she ran out of the room.

I wasn't quite sure what she meant, but I figured it would have to wait until after Bible study was done.

I heard our back door opening and lots of footsteps coming down the hall. Our guests had arrived, and I still needed to get ready. I quickly changed my shirt and ran a brush through my hair and walked out into the living room. The adults and kids were all standing around talking. One of the other moms asked my oldest daughter where I was at. I walked close enough to hear the conversation just in time.

"Oh, she's in the bathroom. She was just putting popsicles in her bum bum; she's going to tell me all about it later after you guys leave."

The entire group froze and looked up at me. Mortified, I looked in confusion at my daughter. The other moms and dads were waiting for my response, trying to hold back their laughter. Awesome, I'm so glad I'm making a great impression, I thought to myself.

"Honey, what in the world are you talking about? Why would you think that Mommy would do something like that?"

I was holding my breath, along with everyone else in the room, as we waited for my daughter to answer.

"Well, you always keep some chocolate in the laundry room. You always tell me I can't have any and that it's 'just for Mommy.' And then I saw you take something out of that blue box under your sink. When you buy it at the store, you always tell me that it's 'just for Mommy,' too. And they look just like the popsicles you buy for us at the store. So I finally figured it out!

You hide special popsicles under your sink, and you put them in your bum bum. And someday when I'm bigger, I'm going to do that, too!"

I stood with my jaw dropped onto the floor. The room erupted with laughter, and my daughter ran out of the room, as she asked her other little friend, "Does your Mommy put popsicles in her bum bum, too?"

Dumbfounded, I shook my head and told our new friends that contrary to my daughter's story, I didn't put popsicles in my rear and that I don't have a hidden stash of them under my bathroom sink. I explained that I had started my period and she must have mistaken the shape of the wrapper for a Popsicle, just like the ones she had been eating all summer long.

I tried to brush the conversation off as we started our Bible study, but I was just still so embarrassed. I had hoped that this new Bible study was going to be a good fit for us and a way to make some new friends. I had almost forgotten about this little incident, when we were standing at the back door saying goodbye, one of the husbands in the group patted me on the back saying, "Goodnight Lauren, don't go and eat too many popsicles this week."

Oh, and our Bible study is still going strong three years later.

PUBLIC RESTROOMS: A VERY SPECIFIC KIND OF TORTURE
AMY WEATHERLY

"To be honest, I'm just winging it. Life, Motherhood, but not my eyeliner because it's Tuesday and I'm not wearing any makeup." ~Amy Weatherly, Writer

"I really have to go to the bathrooooooom!" he shouted as we began the process of unloading and unbuckling to get inside the grocery store to get the one item we needed. Seriously, we only needed ONE. I call it a process because getting out of the car can span anywhere from three minutes to thirty minutes. You never really know whether your kids are in Superman-mode or sloth-mode.

My stomach just sank.

Do you know how hard it is to use a public restroom when you have three kids who are all five and under? HARD. It's very, very hard. And not to mention friggin' disgusting. The germs. It's like a really bad Febreeze commercial-type nightmare.

"Pee or poop?" I asked, silently crossing my fingers it was just a number one type of emergency, and he could pee discreetly on one of my car tires right there in the parking lot.

"BOTH!"

Dang it!!!!! Ohhhhhhh ok. Deep breaths. Here we go.

We run in, baby crying and slipping off my hip, diaper bag falling off my left shoulder, all holding hands shuffling through the parking lot with me singing "Just keep holding, just keep holding, holding, holding."

So we rush inside, make it to the restroom, and there is a worker, mop in hand, ready to clean. The bright orange cone has already been placed outside the door. No, heck no. Not on my watch. We are using this restroom, mister.

"Can we use this restroom really quickly?" I begged him.

"Sure, he answered politely.

So my middle son goes into one stall, while my oldest, my baby and I cram into the stall next to it.

He has requested some "poopacy," which...I don't know why I feel obliged to grant him. I am never ever given the same respect in return...but whatever. When you have kids, the restroom becomes like a family affair.

"What are you doing, mom?"

"Training for the 2022 Winter Olympics in Beijing. I think I'm going to go for Snowboarding freestyle this time, so I really need to practice this 'Air to Fakie' thing if I'm going to make the team. Seriously...what do you think I'm doing? We are together twenty-two hours, seven days a week, leave me alone, for the love of Apple Jacks."

"I mean, I love you and all, but give momma some space."

He's made it pretty clear he doesn't want any help. Four-year-olds rarely do. I still quiver to this day thinking about that bare bottom sitting on that germ-infested throne, but when you've got to go, well you've just got to.

He promised me he put toilet paper down on the seat before using it. This is one of those times where ignorance is bliss, and it's better to take them at their word. Even if you know their word is complete crap.

So anyway, I am trying to pee, holding a baby on my lap. My oldest son was asking a bajillion questions because that's what oldest kids do. We pray for intelligent children. We pray for curious minds - AND THEN WE GET THEM - and we pray for good deals on earplugs from Amazon because of the words. Oh my word, the words. The sheer volume is alarming.

The average person speaks twenty thousand words a day? Bahahahaha please, my kid gets that mess done before my second cup of coffee. I start answering every question with "uh huh, sure." Have I just agreed to eating dessert before dinner? Taking them to Chuck E. Cheese this weekend (Skeeball - woohoo!)? Have I just taught him that Tyrannosaurus-Rex's are still alive and roaming out in the wild? I have no idea because my ears have been turned off since question three. Whatever it is, I'm pretty sure I'll hear more about it later.

Ok, so I'm peeing. My son is jib-jabbing like it's going out of style. I'm trying to hold a baby and pull up my skinny jeans with one hand (which is no easy feat being that I can baaaaarely shimmy them over my muffin top anymore, even first thing in the morning lying flat on my bed).

I gently ask what's going on next door, and my son replies with "still pooping," so I take a quick peek under the stall and notice that this sweet child of mine. This precious son that I prayed for and gave birth to and nursed and rocked and sang sweet lullabies to has taken off every piece of clothing he had been wearing: shirt, jacket, underwear, pants, socks, shoes. They are all scattered everywhere on that nasty gray tile floor.

In the middle of leaning over, I lose my grip on the baby who has silently slithered unharmed and undeterred into the pooping stall with her brother. This is not ideal.

He won't get off the pot to unlock the door for me, because of course, he won't. So at this point, I have to crawl my body under the bathroom stall to get in there, rescue the baby, and find out what the heck is going on. I still have no clue why my kid is butt-naked in this dirty, public restroom. I know it's dirty because the employee is still patiently waiting to clean it outside the door. Poor guy. I just know his mop is all dried out by now. The good news, I guess, is that by the time we get out of there, he will probably be ready for retirement and a life spent with toes in the sand in sunny Pensacola, Florida.

Y'all. I can't explain the mess that was in that bathroom stall. I can't explain it, and I don't want to think about it.

I don't know what to do at this point, but I am mad, embarrassed, and just crazy flustered. So I get my son dressed and cleaned off. And I start attempting to wipe off the toilet, all the while the baby is crawling all over the floor, the boys are wrestling around, and I am yelling "Act normal! Just act like normal people for two seconds!" at the very tippy top of my lungs.

The boys have crashed into the trash can, instead of washing their hands, they are splashing water back and forth at each other, and the baby has made her way back under the stall and is playing in the toilet in the next stall, like, actually playing in it. If I knew how to type out throwing-up-in-my-mouth-a-little sounds right here, I would. They belong in this story.

I have dirty toilet paper up to my elbows from trying to clean the stall. And I'm moaning and groaning and rolling my eyes out loud and just on the verge of losing all my chill. Obviously, the toilet won't flush, because it's just not the day for things actually working and going according to plan.

A minimum of twenty minutes has passed. And all I want is to get out of this hell hole that is the public restroom. And to give that poor guy a raise.

I throw the toilet paper away, I wash everyone's hands up to their shoulders twice, grab my diaper bag and all of its spilled contents up from off the floor, straighten out my shirt, take a deep breath and try to regain an ounce of composure. I walk out of the door with my head held high, give the employee an "I'm-so-sorry-you-have-to-go-in-there" nod, and walk on only to be met by a woman I recognize standing right there.

"Hi, Amy."

Crud. She recognized me.

She heard everything. There's a good chance everyone in the store did. I've never in my life been so dang embarrassed to make eye contact with someone in my entire life. All my dignity - gone like the last bite of ice cream on a hot summer day.

I still never got a clear understanding of why my middle son felt the urge to be naked while he used the restroom to poop that day, and I probably never will. The best answer I got was "I dunno, it just makes me sweaty to poop." Still...let's keep our socks on k, bud?

I filled up my shopping cart with items we didn't need. I loaded in boxes of Organic bunny crackers, ice cream sandwiches, and enough applesauce to feed a military base silently hoping that my large tab would somehow make up for the chaos my family caused in the women's restroom that afternoon. Maybe if I spend a small fortune, they'll have enough to give all of their employees a bonus. Heaven knows, that guy deserves one.

And I have never ever been back since. It will be a long, long time until I'm ready to face that place again.

Using public toilets with young kids is a special and very specific kind of torture.

Seriously, if you make it in and out of there without somebody crawling underneath the stalls or taking off their shoes or wrestling with their brother and knocking each other into the trash can or unlocking your door so everyone and their great-grandmother can see you without your pants on - Bravo! Job well done.

I was not so lucky. Not that day.

THE "RAUR RAURS" ARE COMING
TIFFANY O'CONNOR

"Raising toddlers means that the same three-year-old that screamed 'No Nappy' for three hours in the afternoon will take one bite of food and fall asleep at the dinner table just to be wide awake at two in the morning digging in the freezer trying to find a 'pop-i-cul' (popsicle)." ~#Lifewithboys

When my youngest son was three years old, he had a love-hate relationship with dinosaurs or "Raur Raurs" as he called them. He enjoyed watching television shows about dinosaurs, making me read him the same book about dinosaurs twenty million times, playing with his dinosaur toys in the bathtub, and riding on his Playskool animatronic dinosaur. However, he was also terrified of dinosaurs. He believed that thunder was the sound of dinosaurs roaring and would hide under his blankets anytime there was a thunderstorm. I tried to explain to him that thunder was the sound that lightning makes...but he wasn't having it, and he wouldn't believe me. He was adamant that thunder meant the "Raur Raurs" were coming.

One hot late summer evening in August we were sitting on the front porch stairs, and I was talking to a group of neighbors while my little man ran around the front yard and made a mess with a container of bubbles. Overnight storms were predicted in the forecast and lightning could already be seen in the sky from a distance. When my little man heard the first crack of thunder, he dropped his bubbles on the sidewalk and grabbed my hand and tried to pull me up the stairs towards the door.

"Mama, the Raur Raurs are coming. Go inside time."

"OK, go inside baby. I will follow you in a second." I told him and then turned back to my conversation with the other adults…a luxury that I rarely got to enjoy.

He kept pulling on my arm. "Mama, NOW!!! Inside time Mama!!!"

Again I brushed him off and told him to go inside and continued my conversation with our neighbors.

After several ignored protests he crawled up into my lap and put his little hands on both sides of my cheeks and pulled my face close to his and looked me dead in the eyes.

I was not prepared for what he was about to say. Never in a million years would I have ever guessed what words were about to come out of that angelic cherub looking toddler's mouth.

He looked me in the eyes with his hands on my cheeks and his nose against mine. His eyebrows furrowed into a scowl and his icy blue eyes intently focused on mine. He took a deep breath and said,

"Bitch! The Raur Raurs are coming. Go inside NOW!!!"

I was immediately mortified and honestly really confused. Had I heard him correctly? Did my baby boy just call me a bitch? Where in the world had he learned to use that word that way? Why would he call me that?

CRAP! Did the neighbors hear him?

I looked up, and they were all looking at us. A few of them were giggling and were obviously amused. A couple of them were looking at me in horror while they probably judged my horrible parenting skills.

I immediately started regretting all of my sketchy parenting decisions like watching R-rated movies or listening to rap when my children were present. I should have known better. I should have realized they would soak up all of the profanity like little sponges.

My son couldn't tell the difference between the colors green and blue yet, but apparently, he could use four-letter words like an obscenity champ.

What happened next was a blur. I yelled at him for saying such a naughty curse word, and I think I might have threatened to wash his dirty little mouth out with soap like the mom in A Christmas Story. I asked him where he had heard that word from and why he would call me that.

"I sorry I was the bads Mama…but Raur Raurs ARE coming." He said with his little bottom lip quivering and tears starting to well up in his eyes.

I told him never to use that word again, bathed him, and put him to bed.

"I love you, Mama. I don't want the Raur Raurs to eat you up." He said as I kissed him goodnight. He was still bothered by our interaction outside earlier. I was a little bothered too, but I hugged him close, kissed his forehead, and told him that I loved him and that everything would be ok.

The next morning he woke me up with the biggest grin on his face. "Mama comes wit me" he screeched. I followed him to the back door, and there in our back yard was a giant tree limb. Lighting had severed it during the storm, and it had landed near his swing set.

"See Mama I told you the Raur Raurs were coming. The Raur Raurs stepped on the tree and made it go boom boom (He made stomping motions with his feet) I saved you like Spiderman, Mama. I NOT the bads." He proclaimed triumphantly. "The Raur Raurs are the bads!"

During the toddler years, you will experience many firsts with your child... unfortunately sometimes that includes their first bad word. On the bright side, my youngest son is ten now, and I have not heard him call anyone else a bitch since that day...however, I do have to remind him not to call his older brother a shit head or say the word fuck from time to time, so we are not exactly out of the expletive woods yet.

GROCERY SHOPPING WITH TODDLERS IS SO MUCH FUN!
DIANA KANE

"Who needs a gym when you get this kind of exercise trying to buy groceries?"~ Mama Needs a Cupcake

How can you make grocery shopping more fun you ask? Well, let me tell you! Just throw a couple screaming kids into your cart and challenge yourself to come home with more than two items on your list. It is so much fun! I can't wait for you to try it!

Are you excited about frequent shopper miles at the good ol' grocery store? You should be! Those fools are going to have the pleasure of your business on a daily basis!

If you thought dragging one screaming child into a grocery store was fun… just wait till you have two heathens to lug into such establishments. It is a total blast! For real, this is the stuff parents' dream of. By the time you get the big one in the back of the cart and the short one up front, there's really no point in even being at the grocery store. Pushing two kids in a cart while balancing a box of diapers on your head and shoving a box of tampons between your boobs because there is zero room in the cart for anything else isn't a super effective way to grocery shop. It is way fun though, I can't wait for you to try it!

Before you get your panties in a bunch trying to get out the door, I would like to pass on a little bit of advice that I have been gifted from some veteran mamas. Steal the magical parking spot adjacent to the cart return. It's a Life Changer! Or if you are at one of those fancy establishments they have these special parking spots up close for expectant mothers. I expect a lot out of my children so I always nab that space if I can! It completely eliminates having to choose between leaving your kids in the car while sprinting back to the cart return or dragging them kicking and screaming on the sixty-yard dash back to the vehicle. Plus, CPS kind of frowns on unattended children so you are totally covered! But, you will need to make sure you brush off the side of your car so everyone knows exactly where to aim when they give the old twenty-foot heave-ho and smash their cart into the side of your vehicle. It is totally fine though. Those new plastic carts don't do near the damage.

If you are as fortunate as I am to have a magician in the family, once you have procured a parking spot, you will need to refocus your efforts on redressing your child. You know the one that removes all of their clothing while strapped into a five-point harness. So stinking proud of those kids! Don't forget to spend at least three extra minutes locating their shoes because if they venture into the store without shoes on it completely eliminates your opportunity to backtrack all of your footsteps while in the store after they throw them off. This really is probably my favorite part of any grocery trip.

Upon complying with the no shirt, no shoes standards…you can strut straight through those sliding glass doors to secure all the necessary ingredients to prepare that home-cooked meal you have been craving for months! Unless that is your child is doing the whole sometimes I potty on the potty thing. Then like us, you will need to make a quick pit stop to the frog potty located in the back of your SUV. Store potties simply will not do, because they don't sing to you upon urination. It's a total bummer!

I personally like to try and disguise the fact that my child is peeing in the back of my car by pretending to have an intelligent conversation on the phone with no one on the other end. But if you prefer to do the potty dance with your child, more power to you.

Next, you will need to discretely dump the pee on the backside of the tire and jump over the stream as it rolls back toward you. It's really an art form that takes a lot of practice…but you'll get it!

Once you finally make it into the store, make sure you allow your kids to crawl into one of those extended seat carts. You know, the kind that has an extra row positioned in front of the cart for you to "put" things in. Most states require a CDL to drive this monstrosity and you likely won't be able to go down most aisles…but they are totally worth it!

Now, wait approximately five seconds after you have buckled your small children into the "happy" mobile that they were making such a fuss over for them to fully morph into screaming unrecognizable creatures. It is truly incredible what toddlers can do these days, you know?! This will become your first trial in pushing the massive cart quickly to the snack bar. Be careful though, those things are super heavy and you could totally pop those hemorrhoids out! Once you reach the snack bar don't be overwhelmed by all of the options. You really should just stick to the popcorn and a slushy so they can later spill it all over aisle four and cause you to slip and strain that special area that you asked the doctor to put a few extra stitches in wink* wink*.

Are you ready to get your grocery shopping on?!

Head straight for the milk and diapers, because that is all you are actually going to make it out with. Don't be deterred by your newly found masters of seatbelt buckling and unbuckling. They are just now getting the hang of this whole gross motor skills thing and it's really good for them to get in and out of their seat at least 262 times before you successfully leave the store. Plus, every time you return a child to their seat you will be delighted to notice that there will be a few new random items in your cart. For bulk shopping, it is best to park your cart in the cereal aisle so your offspring can indulge in all those super healthy sugar cereals that cause them to act like complete maniacs.

Also, make sure to run into one of your friends from a previous life that doesn't have kids! You know the one that isn't dressed like a homeless person and has organic everything in their cart...oh and coupons. They always remember to bring the coupons that they cut out. It may be difficult to look upon someone shopping with such ease...but trust me; they are having a way harder time looking at you.

You will officially know it is time to head towards the check out once the baby has successfully opened a bottle of barbeque sauce and the toddler has chewed a hole through the top corner of the box of Lucky Charms. They are magically delicious.

Upon surrender, you will likely be sporting a child under your armpit squirming for dear life while pushing the fifty-pound cart with the other. This is usually when the additional child seizes the opportunity to empty the rest of an applesauce squeeze onto the floor. You will likely slip and do one of those I kind of rolled my ankle things, but I can still walk on it while the child under your armpit cancels out your card number six times before you finally get a receipt.

Oh man, shopping with toddlers is so much fun, but don't worry! You will get the chance to do it again tomorrow because all you ended up buying was milk, diapers and a whole bunch of crappy cereal!

ARE YOU SMARTER THAN A TODDLER?
STEPHANIE ORTIZ

"The shortest distance between two points is a straight line. The longest distance (and the loudest wail) is between a toddler's head and the neck opening of a shirt." ~Six Pack Mom

Raising toddlers requires a tremendous amount of patience, energy, & paper towels. Paper towels are key because when you run out of both patience and energy, your toddler will likely seize that very moment to slip away undetected, just long enough to create a gargantuan spill or mess that requires said paper towels.

Now as a mother of six children, I figured I'd mastered the art of parenting a toddler... until my youngest son came along. My youngest forced me to up my parenting game considerably, mainly by performing all sorts of impish shenanigans when given the slightest opportunity to do so. Countless times I've tearfully confessed to my husband, "I don't know what to do with this kid; he's scary smart. I mean SCARY."

Staying one step ahead of him requires me to stay even more focused than I already was as a parent. One of the casualties of this vigilance is my phone use. Being distracted for any lengthy period of time is a liability with my little guy, so my phone is cast aside for much of the day.

But in this one particular case, I couldn't be more thankful that I happened to have my phone on my person.

Recently, our toddler outgrew his crib. I say "outgrew," because it sounds a lot better than saying he had taken to "swinging himself up and out of the crib like a tiny jet-propulsion engine."

We tried various methods of containment, but the inevitable was upon us. It was the end of the crib era, or rather, the dawning era of the toddler bed.

Gone were the days of plopping him into his crib for a nap and taking some time to relax (and by "relax," I mean "folding laundry," or "not fishing toothbrushes out of the toilet." Toddler naptime soon became a period of repeatedly entering the room, with stern admonishments of varying decibels to "stay in bed."

My son initially took that to mean: "DESTROY every inch of your room first, including your bed, but stay on it."

He would loiter around his room, and eventually end up falling fast asleep anywhere BUT in the bed. But no worries- he was at least in his room, right?

Until one day....

Unbeknownst to us, the door to our son's room was in need of repair; the hinges were cracked, which left the door slightly askew. After a few repeated toddler escapes, my husband resorted to placing a childproof plastic door knob protectors on the doorknob inside our son's room, discouraging him from opening the door.

It seemed like an appropriate deterrent, until he somehow opened the door at two in the morning.

The Unofficial Guidebook to Surviving Life With Toddlers

Have you ever been awakened at two in the morning by a mysterious, child-like apparition standing at your bedside, reeking of peanut butter? I have. It's alarming, but not nearly as alarming as when the child hugs you with his peanut butter-coated body, and you realize that your bedroom was not the first stop on his peanut butter snack excursion tour.

(It's been months, and I still find peanut butter remnants in random locations of the house. Today it was inside the DVD player, people. INSIDE IT.)

The toddler's nocturnal ramblings required us to enter phase two of bedroom security- TOTAL LOCKDOWN. My husband reversed the doorknob, so we could lock the door from the outside and keep our son safely secured in his bedroom at night. I was genuinely relieved to secure him in bed that night, assured that both the peanut butter and the toddler would remain contained.

Six minutes after his last cup of water and tuck into bed, the door creaked open, and out popped our triumphant toddler, bounding proudly into the living room.
Again.
And again.
And again.
I even tried placing the plastic childproof knob cover on the inside of the door AND locking the door. Still, he managed to bust our crack security measures & pop out proudly.

Remember in "Jurassic Park" when the velociraptors were hunting the kids hiding in the kitchen? The kids closed the door, certain they'd be safe, because there's no way that a raptor could open a door, right? Wrong. Well, our tiny raptor of a boy had somehow figured out how to open a door that was LOCKED. And for an exhausted mom, that's just as frightening as a velociraptor loose.

There were tears as he was punished for repeatedly breaking and exiting (?) when told to stay in bed. He got the message: no more unlocking the door.

Finally, I scooped him up and carried him into his bedroom, securing the door firmly behind us in the dark. I stroked his head, sang to him, and gingerly crept toward the door. I squeezed the plastic door knob protector quietly to open it, and... Nothing.

The knob wouldn't turn.

The door was locked from the outside.

Apparently, unbeknownst to me, my son had managed to jiggle his door within the hinges just right to open it without actually unlocking it. By closing the door behind us, I'd managed to lock us in.

As I sat in the dark pondering how to get myself out, I also realized one critical issue:

I had to pee.

What to do? My own bedroom was right next door, but my pounding on the wall did nothing to awaken my husband, who sleeps like the dead. Staying locked in all night was not an option, because like I said, PEE.

The room was pitch-black. The plastic doorknob cover was still on. I scrambled to pry it off, but I couldn't even see where the clips met. No matter how many times I fiddled with it, I simply couldn't get the cover to pop off.

I paused to debate strategies- should I open the window and hop out? No, if the toddler caught me, he'd absolutely do it next time, too. Should I curl up in the toddler's bed with him & call it a night? Anyone who's ever slept with their child in a toddler bed knows that within an hour, your spine will cry in protest.

It was dark. And stuffy. The room felt smaller somehow. Yup. I still had to pee.

In desperation, I even woke up my son, by asking him to help me unlock the door. I also ate a big old helping of shame as he blinked and said in his sweet toddler voice, "But Mama, you said I can't unlock the door."
Oh. OH.
But as luck would have it, I realized that my phone was on his dresser. So I was able to phone a friend- by dialing my own house number.
My ear cupped to the wall between our bedrooms; I heard the ring, then another ring, then...

Husband: "uhhh ughafhjfakf uh hulllllo?"
Me: "It's me (like I NEEDED to clarify that??). I'm stuck in the toddler's room."

THAT'S when you know you've been married for a long time.
Because my husband didn't ask me why. Or how. Or speak at all. He merely lumbered to the door, unlocked it, turned, and limped drowsily back into bed.

Thankfully, my son was too exhausted from witnessing his mom's stupidity to do anything but fall fast asleep. But the next day, during naptime, he called me from his room with the door STILL locked. He'd transferred the plastic childproof ("adult-proof," apparently) knob from his bedroom door onto his closet door, all "by mesef!"

Am I smarter than a fifth grader? I used to think so. Am I smarter than a toddler? Apparently not.

But at least I can phone a friend.

NOTES FROM THE GRAND BEDTIME EXPERIMENT

SHANNON BRESCHER SHEA

"The fear when you wake up and realize you fell asleep in your toddler's room- BUT THEY NEVER DID." ~We'll Eat You Up, We Love You So

Sleep deprivation? Check. Bizarre, illogical requests? Check. Not understanding what is required of you? Check.

Parenting often feels like a psychological experiment where we're both the researcher and the subject. That was never more apparent to me than the night we switched our three-year-old from a crib to a toddler bed. While we knew it was going to be bad, even we couldn't predict the results.

Hypothesis: The three-year-old will eventually stay in bed if you walk him back enough times.

Procedure: Tuck the child into a new toddler bed. Walk him back to bed every time he gets up.

The Unofficial Guidebook to Surviving Life With Toddlers

Results:

8:00 PM: Lab conditions are set. The subject's sibling has been secured in his crib and has entered REM.

8:30 PM: The researcher tucks the subject in bed, kisses his forehead, and says, "Goodnight, don't let the bedbugs bite, sleep tight, I love you."

8:31 PM: The researcher retreats to the couch to await results. While this experiment has been tried many times before, they have all been in other families. She anticipates that this particular child will bring forth new and "exciting" results.

8:32 PM: Before the researcher has fully rested her bottom on the couch, the subject has emerged from his sleeping quarters. He is looking for "something." The subject refuses to specify what that "something" is. He wanders the room, staring at the ceiling. He takes a toy off the bookshelf and moves it from hand to hand. The researcher rises from the couch and walks him back to bed.

8:33 PM: The subject sticks his head out of his room, peering into the adjacent living room. "Yes?" the researcher asks — the subject retreats.

8:35 PM: The researcher feels it is safe to put on the electric kettle. She is wrong. The subject slams open his door and sprints across the living room. She chases after him and grabs his hand. Together, they walk back through the door. She tucks him into bed.

8:37 PM-9:20 PM: The subject runs out of his room approximately twenty more times. Much of the time, he is already up before the researcher has left the room. The researcher and co-researcher take turns accompanying him back to his sleeping quarters. There is some disagreement over this, with each person saying, "It's your turn," no matter whose turn it actually is.

9:25 PM: Approximately the twenty-first time the subject has left the room, he shouts, "Now you follow me!" He giggles violently. Although the researcher knows this is a serious process, she cracks a smile behind her hand. She manages to hold back a laugh.

9:30 PM: The researchers suspect it may be worth pursuing an alternative process. The co-researcher says to the subject, "If you run out again, we'll have to put up a baby gate." The researcher is appalled that her partner would consider such a breach in ethics. She makes a very disapproving face. The subject bursts out in tears. Although she rarely does so, the researcher contradicts her partner. She insists that they will most certainly not put up a baby gate tonight. The subject stops crying. He then sprints back out of the room. Both researchers sigh.

9:30 PM-10:00 PM: The subject runs out of his room approximately ten more times. The researchers return him to his room and tuck him back into bed every time.

10:05 PM: The researcher becomes convinced that they must be following the experimental procedure wrong. Her voice cracks as she asks her partner, "How do we deal with this?" He throws up his hands and responds, "I don't know!" She double-checks the instructions on the internet. According to the best psychologists, the child should get bored and stay in bed after getting up thirty times or more. The researcher suspects they have already passed that point.

10:10 PM-10:30 PM: The subject runs out of his room approximately ten more times. The researchers return him to his room and tuck him back into bed every time.

10:45 PM: The researcher wonders if connecting with the subject on a personal level would help. She asks, "Are you afraid of bad dreams?" He shakes his head yes. "I have bad dreams sometimes. Everyone does. You know, Pop [the researcher's father] sleepwalks. One time, he walked over to the fridge in the middle of the night. Nana [the researcher's mother] asked him what he was looking for and he said, "Farts!" Both the researcher and the subject laugh. She hopes this has reassured the subject enough to keep him in bed. However, the researcher notices that the subject doesn't look any sleepier than he did at the beginning of the experiment. She yawns.

10:46 PM: The subject runs back out of his room. He stops at the refrigerator and yells, "Farts!" The researcher regrets sharing that information with him.

10:46 PM-11:47 PM: The subject runs out of his room twenty-eight times in a single hour. The researchers wonder if they are the ones being tested, not the subject. They have started to hallucinate. They keep imagining that the child is in bed when he is, in fact, standing in front of them yet again.

11:48 PM: The researchers give up on the experiment. It is clear that they have either followed the directions wrong or the subject is extraordinarily talented. Either way, it is clear who is in control. It is not the researchers.

The regular courses of action have failed. All efforts have failed. There is no recourse but to shut it all down.

11:50 PM: The researchers retreat to their bedroom. They are done for the day. Maybe for the year. They seriously question if they are cut out for the science of parenting.

11:51 PM: The subject refuses to end the experiment. He approaches the bed, much to the researchers' surprise. "You're in pajamas," he states. The researcher looks over at his blond head and replies, "Yes, I know." She walks him back to bed.

11:52 PM: The researchers have shut down the lab and closed all of the doors. The subject returns to the side of the bed. "It's dark in the house," he says. The researcher has nothing left to say. She stares at him. Finally, she says, "Go to bed." The subject finally obeys.

The laboratory is quiet. The house is still. A baby cries.

Conclusion: The researchers strongly recommend not pursuing this line of research. Further investigation reveals that just sitting with the child in his room is a far more effective course of action. They recommend that other researchers do whatever works for them, "proper" procedure be damned.

WIPE MY BUTT
SHANNON CARPENTER

"A lot of parenting books give advice that is completely useless like, 'when traveling by yacht make sure the toddler is polite to the help.' Who actually parents on a yacht? That's what the help is for." ~ Hossman at Home.

"Wipe my butt," my three-year-old, Ollie, says.

"No."

"Wipe my butt."

"No! I'm done wiping butts," I tell him.

"Wipe! My! Butt!"

I have three children. And because of proper family planning, I have been dealing with diapers and butt wiping for a solid eight years. I had a magical year when I didn't have to change any diapers or wipe any butts. It was right before my youngest was born, but my middle son was potty trained.

He could wipe his own butt. But other than that one glorious year, I have been the chief poop dealer. I'm done.

"Daddy!" Ollie says. "You wipe my butt!" The way he says it is all smarmy and laced with contempt. The ending 'T' is said hard and with spittle. Look at little Mr. Big Shot here. He gets his bum wiped by the help. His words echo in the small downstairs bathroom like he's in an auditorium giving a speech to the plebes.

"No. I've taught you how to wipe your butt a month ago. Now get wiping. I'm not doing it."

"You wipe my butt!" He then turns around and presents himself to me like some sort of poop peacock.

"Forget it. I'm not wiping your butt. You are a big boy now. Big boys wipe their own butts," I say. I'm using the good old fatherhood cliché of "you're a big boy now." It will work. It always works. I've been an at-home dad for eight years. I know how this game is played.

He bends down further, and his nose is touching his knees.

"Wipe!"

"No!"

This is the way it goes for another five minutes. My toddler was scootching his dirty bum towards me and me moving away. It's a battle of wills. Who has the stronger intestinal fortitude? Who can look at the stink eye and not flinch? I'm not budging. Enough is enough, and I'm tired of dealing with poop. There have been so many diapers. So many things we have peed on. Truck tires, trees, and once off the side of a cliff. I've done the awkward diaper changes in the front seat of my car with my son contorted like he is Cirque Du Soleil--toddler addition. Any place that has a changing table in the men's room has become my favorite.

"Look, buddy," I say, switching tactics. I'm going for the best friend approach. The big boy thing isn't working. "You have to do this. It's part of growing up." He turns to look at me. His little brow is furrowed, and please let that tongue sticking out mean he is deep in thought and not trying to push out something else.

"No, Daddy," he finally says. "Wipe my butt."

"All your friends are wiping their own butts," I tell him. I have no idea if this is true or not. I make it a habit not to go into bathrooms with kids that are not my own. "Audra wipes her own butt. She's great at it. Audra is a butt wiping machine. Wipes all day long. Do you know what she does first thing in the morning?"

"What?" he says. "Wipes her own butt. No she doesn't," he says and laughs.

"Yup. I talked to her dad. She wipes before breakfast. Don't you want to be like Audra?"

I've got him now. Audra is his best friend. She is a cute little girl that comes to playgroup. They run and yell and discuss proper butt-wiping techniques.

Ollie doesn't say anything for a moment. More thinking.

"Wipe my butt!" Ollie says and then smashes his foot against the floor.

"No!" I say.

"Yes!!"

"NO!!!"

"YES!!!!"

I'm in a screaming match with a toddler. This could be going better. Potty training ends today. No more asking if that brown smudge on my finger is chocolate, and then bringing it up to my nose for the whiff of shame.

"Ok, let's start over," I say. My breathing is a little too heavy, and I'm worked up. How can such a small person do this to me? Oh yeah, the butt wiping thing and how I'm done with it. "I've taught you how to wipe, right? We spent weeks on it. It's just a natural part of growing up. Think about it, this is the next step. Do this, and we are done potty training. So what do you say? How about you wipe your own butt."

Using logic with a three-year-old usually works out well.

"No!" he says.

"Wipe your butt, Christ!"

I'll admit, I lose it a bit. I shouldn't, but I'm just done. Seriously. I'm not touching any more poop. Eight years is long enough. I don't care what the potty training books say. "When your child is ready, they will express interest...." Blah. Blah. Blah. I'm ready, and I'm expressing interest. I've got so much interest that I'm willing to get into a metaphysical debate with a little person that thinks that Rainbow Dash is the greatest My Little Pony. For the record, it's Twilight Sparkle. She's the bomb, and I bet she is fully potty trained.

"That's it!" I say. It's time for the fatherhood nuclear option — the one that is final; no walking back from. "We are done arguing about this. Stay in this bathroom until you wipe your butt. Don't come out until you are clean!" There. FINISHED!

I leave him in the bathroom. I pick up a magazine, and I pretend to read it while I sit on the couch. It's what you do when you are waiting someone out. Look busy and thus important, like you don't have time for shenanigans.

Another five minutes go by. Nothing. And then, I hear it. The flush! There is a flush! We have a flush, people! A FLUSH! Then another one. More flushes follow--a Flushapalooza is happening.

Ollie comes hopping out of the bathroom. His pants are around his ankles so he can't actually take a step. He's all smiles, and that is fantastic. Victory is mine! The poop has been vanquished, and it's time to celebrate.

"Daddy! I wipe my butt! I wipe my butt!" he says.

I'm off the couch and start dancing before I even get to him. I pick him up, naked butt and all, and give him a big hug. We do twirls. There is laughter. It's Mardi Gras time in suburbia. I have a tear in my eye. "My big boy!" I say. "My big boy!" Hugs and kisses, flushes and toilet paper, clean underwear and clean butts. We have made it to the Promised Land.

"I did it! I did it! I did it lots of times!"

"Wait, what?" I ask.

"I wiped my butt. Then I wiped my butt again, and again, and again!"

And there, ladies and gentlemen is my mistake. The flaw in my plan. With my half-naked son still in my arms, I go back into the bathroom. My first step splashes in the water on the floor. Things have gone wrong. It smells mildewy in here. There is lots of water with stuff in it. Scientists call this an "overflowed toilet."

"Good job, bud, "I say, not wanting to take away from my son's victory. "Now we are going to teach you how to plunge a toilet."

"No!" he says.

I'm done wiping butts, but I'm not done dealing with poop.

KNICK-KNOCK JOKES
JACKIE PICK

"My kids' jokes are terrible, but at least it takes them forever to tell them" ~Jackie Pick, Writer

I nicknamed my twin boys "Woody" and "Buzz" while I was pregnant with them and would serenade my belly with "You've Got a Friend in Me."

They've been trying to get back at me ever since.

One Saturday morning when they were not-quite-three, the boys woke at five in the morning with their usual comedy routine. They'd fallen in love with knock-knock jokes – or "Knick-knock" as they said it – and began their days telling one or ten of them. This morning, they got as far as "Knick-knock," before they dissolved in laughter, then loudly plotted how best to nab the box of donuts I'd put on a high shelf. Their plan was to carb load on forbidden donuts and then play with their plastic bowling set on the hardwood floor right outside my bedroom.

My husband and I groaned. This was not the gentle family weekend wakeup we'd dreamed of since learning we'd be parents. This was more of a donut-fueled, pre-dawn, terrible Big Lebowski remake.

Moments later, the boys were setting up pins and raring to go. Between arguing about rules, they bowled, releasing the ball with a cry that sounded like a troupe of overly excited howler monkeys. Ball, pins, and the occasional child rammed against my bedroom door every few moments.

"Children are the worst alarm clocks," my husband said and buried his head under a pillow.

"Hey," I said oh-so romantically. "I need to talk with you before things get much crazier this morning. Let me just quiet the boys up."

I stumbled out of bed and opened the door at the exact moment the boys decided they were going to turn themselves into human bowling balls. They double-somersaulted into me, causing me to topple onto the bowling set.

"She got a spare!" As the boys jumped around, it was hard to tell where one ended and the other began. They were a palindrome of limbs, giggles, and purloined donut crumbs.

Buzz grabbed my hand. "Knick-knock!"

"Jokes later. Right now I want to talk to daddy for a few minutes. Will you please go in the family room?" They nodded solemnly, then ran off towards certain shenanigans and likely property damage.

Carefully stepping over bowling pins and something sticky I didn't even bother to try to identify, I went back into the bedroom. "Honey, I wanted –"

My husband released a mighty snore. Awake and now on-duty, I went out to see what mayhem was brewing with the boys.

"Where ya going, Magellan?" I asked, my arched eyebrow indicating something between a warning and curiosity.

The boys, now frozen, were on tippy-toes at the front door, trying to undo the deadbolt.

We'd installed the extra lock because whenever they thought we weren't looking, the twins liked to go see if our neighbors were home by running over to their porch and pressing their little noses to their kitchen door. I'd caught them mid-jail break. Also mid-dress: Woody wore boxer shorts and one snow boot. Buzz was naked except for a strip of toilet paper stuck to his foot.

"It's far too early to visit the neighbors, and you are far too naked."

In an act of fraternal selflessness, Woody offered Buzz the underpants he was wearing and the two once again ran off to plan their next getaway attempt.

I started cleaning up the kitchen where the boys had ripped open the donut box like jackals when I heard a muted, "Mama!"

"What?!!" I hollered delicately and maternally.

"Mama!" Still muffled.

We played this strange version of Marco Polo – Mama! What? – as I sought the source. Finally, I wandered toward the back stairs.

Behold! Woody's head was stuck in the banister. He looked perplexed but otherwise unharmed.

Proving he is both opportunistic and situationally tone deaf, Buzz stuck his eager face right into Woody's.

"Knick-knock!"

"No, Buzz! Go away!"

I sent Buzz to get his father because this particular situation was beyond both my skill level and my pay grade. My husband eventually meandered out from the bedroom, looked at Woody's head, paused, then declared, "I'll get the Crisco."

As Woody probably got into this situation because he often uses his hair as a napkin, I didn't think more lubrication would help.

My only training for Large Head in Small Spaces crises was my prenatal classes, but that was enough. "His head is the biggest part of his body. Everything else must follow."

We turned Woody's body ninety degrees and whoosh! It's a boy! Woody emerged unharmed, aside from his post-emancipation hairdo.

"Are you ok?" my husband asked.

Woody nodded, then asked, "Daddy, can I get a Band-Aid?"

"Sure, buddy."

He smiled and leaned in close to my face. "Mama?"

"Yes, sweetie?"

"Knick-knock."

We all jumped at that moment because someone actually knocked at the door. I looked incredulously at the clock – 6:02 AM.

My husband and I went to answer the door, encouraging Woody to find the Band-Aids in our bathroom and have at it.

We opened the door to see our neighbor in his bathrobe. His hands rested on the shoulders of a small, familiar-looking boy who was quite naked except for his brother's underpants and a piece of toilet paper stuck to his foot.

"This is yours, yes?" Our neighbor smiled.

It seems Buzz finally figured out the deadbolt.

In the hubbub of Woody's head being stuck, I hadn't noticed Buzz's absence. He'd snuck out and predictably pressed his nose against our neighbor's sliding glass door. Fortunately, they have children of their own, so they were general unfazed at the early morning visit from Peeping Buzz.

Still, my cheeks burned. "I'm so sorry."

Our neighbor waved it off, "They're welcome anytime." He winked at Buzz. "Just, you know, after 9 AM."

"Thank you," Buzz and I chorused.

My husband walked the neighbor out, engaging him in a conversation about the fine art of mulching.

I turned around to talk with Buzz about safety and privacy, but Woody was already there, covered head to toe in the overnight maxi pads he'd mistaken for Band-Aids.

"How fast did you go, Buzz?"

"So fast! I saw our neighbors eat pancakes!"

"Yeah." Woody stared at Buzz with respect. "You win."

My husband returned. "Did you want to talk?" he asked.

I sank onto the couch. "Soon. I just need to sit for a minute."

I closed my eyes and almost fell asleep, but my husband's voice pulled me back towards consciousness.

"Boys, get away from Mommy's nose."

I opened my eyes to several sticky fingers dangerously close to exploring my nostrils. I started to tickle the tummy and toes within reach. No matter who I touched, both squealed. They shrieked and ran off, rough and tumble, elbows and giggles.

"They're exhausting," my husband sighed. He plopped down next to me on the couch and closed his eyes.

"So, is this a bad time to tell you I'm pregnant?" I asked.

My husband's eyes popped open. Before he could utter a word, the boys ran back in and jumped on us, each taking one of our laps.

"Knick-knock, Mama!"

"Who's there?" I asked.

Woody and Buzz looked at each other. They'd never gotten this far in the joke with us and now they were stumped.

My husband and I started laughing, and the boys joined in. In our joy at that terribly early hour, it was impossible to tell where one of us ended and the next one began.

WHAT TO EXPECT AFTER POTTY TRAINING
RITA TEMPLETON

"It's no coincidence that dawdler rhymes with toddler" ~ Fighting Off Frumpy

Potty training is the holy grail of toddler achievements, the magic milestone that anybody who's ever been tired of changing diapers (which is … EVERY PARENT) is desperate to reach. The tinkling of urine against the plastic potty chair is music to a parent's ears. And with the dropping of one tiny turd into the proper receptacle, we dance around in celebration like our kid has just won a Nobel Prize and resist the urge to post triumphantly on social media. (Please, please promise me you resist the urge.) We want to drive through the streets tossing fresh diapers like candy at a parade to those parents still deep in the diapering trenches, because our kid doesn't need them anymore, YAAAAY!

I know this because I've potty trained FOUR children. And I should know better, but each time I've been that excited. Like it's this huge breakthrough. Like it's the end of all the messes I'll have to clean up, ever. Somehow I never consider that "no more diapers" does NOT mean "kid uses the bathroom with complete independence, requiring zero assistance whatsoever EVER AGAIN." Because even when they're "potty trained" (notice those quotation marks), there are several other, equally unpleasant factors to contend with, which in my experience can take literally years to overcome. For example:

THE "UH-OH, MOMMY!"

This is what happens when the kid knows how to use the toilet but doesn't always grasp the timing of getting there. It's what daycare centers and kindly moms refer to as "accidents," and what I refer to as, "Damn it, kid! I don't need any more laundry!" They haven't yet learned to accurately read their body's signals, which often results in either soiled pants or an unsavory trail of ... something, all the way to the bathroom. And even when they're a little older, they sometimes get too engrossed in playing or tormenting their siblings or whatever and bam: Piss City. (Or Diarrhea Town, if you're particularly unlucky.)

THE CLOTHING CONUNDRUM

This is when the kid's out of diapers but still sucks at maneuvering clothing up and down and snapping and zipping and stuff. Sometimes you have to help them pull their pants down. Sometimes you have to help them pull their pants up. Sometimes you forget that they can't pull their pants up which leads to them waddling, bare-butted and junk waving in the breeze, into the living room where you are entertaining company. Sometimes they take their shoes off to get their pants down, which then must be put on again, and we all know how that goes with a toddler. And most of the time, there are buttons and zippers to contend with.

Bonus points if your kid feels he must be completely naked to poop.

THE AIM GAME

This might be a moot point for mothers of girls, but for those of us with kids of the dudely persuasion, it's definitely an issue. Because even when your kid can use the toilet, it takes a long damn time (in some cases, a lifetime) for them to learn to use it successfully. When boys pee, the goal is simple: just hit the water. You'd think this would be an easy task, but no – because there are apparently things to do while you pee that are more important than aiming, like looking around and messing with the flusher and the towel on the rack above the toilet and spraying urine like an unattended firehose in the process. This is to say nothing of the fact that you must remind them on a constant basis to PLEASE. PUT. THE SEAT. DOWN.

... For like six years, possibly longer if you aren't consistent.

THE HYGIENE HASSLE

You think your days of inspecting tiny buttholes for cleanliness are over, but no – because for the foreseeable future, they will need help wiping after they poop. They'll require your assistance (heh ... ass-sistance) for so long that you start to envision yourself wiping their butts as you send them off to college. You'll wonder, "Does my child really need help or is he just being lazy about it?" And then your question will be answered when your kid tries to wipe himself and ends up with poop smeared all over the toilet and down the backs of his legs and in between his fingers. Yes. They need help for eons. And you'll pay dearly if you don't drop everything at once to attend to said butt-wiping – because either they will have made a mess with it, or the poo will have started to dry (it happens fast, trust me) and it will be a spackled-on situation that only an entire box of baby wipes can handle. Don't buy the cheap ones, just saying.

THE PERILS OF PUBLIC PEEING (OR POOPING)

Either way, once your kid realizes that he can use the toilet, the public restrooms of the world become his personal playground. Shopping at Target, the grocery store, the mall, the park, the zoo, the doctor's office, the hardware store, Taco Bell, the White House ... it doesn't matter where you are. If you're away from home, he's going to want to check out the "facilities" – guaranteed. The problem is, you can't just send a barely-potty-trained little person in by themselves and hope for the best. You've got to stop what you're doing and accompany them. To make matters worse, they don't get how nightmarishly disgusting public toilets are, so you're cringing and saying, "No, don't touch that!" and "NO! Don't touch that!" while they are, of course, absolutely touching that. Then you have to wash their hands, which means hoisting them up to a sink they can't reach and getting their sleeves and yours all wet and splashing water all over the place and hoping they don't touch anything with their clean hands while you're fetching paper towels.

See what I'm saying? I don't know why we get so excited about our kids being out of diapers. Because when I think about it, I'd rather spend forty-five seconds changing one (aren't we all pros at this point?) than grapple with most anything else we just discussed. Yeah, they're out of diapers, but so what? We're still virtual slaves to their bodily functions, and "I need help wiping" will haunt our dreams indefinitely. There's no real winner here.

My advice to potential potty-training parents is this: buck the trend, invest in some huge diapers and encourage your kids to use the toilet less. At least until they learn to do it all by themselves, or college, whichever comes first.

BURNING QUESTIONS, NICK. JR. EDITION

JOE MEDLER

"Don't be silly. Of course there's a good reason my toddler is naked! He found a drop of water on his shirt. A DROP OF WATER! ~Developing Dad

Sometime when their child is between the age of three months and a year the sights and sounds of children's television become the droning background of many a parent's existence. At some point, it's just inconsiderate to keep HGTV or ESPN on so we can ignore our little ones so we turn on one of a few channels providing round the clock entertainment for kids of varying ages so they can turn the tables and ignore us for a while. It turns out that they need us so much that a few minutes of being ignored quickly becomes an hour. If you feed them and powder them at some point, you might even get two hours out of it. If you've read this far, you are a parent. If you are a parent, especially one with little ones present or in your recent past, you know that a couple of hours is nothing short of 1980 Olympic Hockey team miraculous.

Before you know it you are humming maddeningly catchy theme songs in the few moments you have to yourself. Or at work, that excellent place where you can get a coffee or take a leak without any logistical issues delaying either. What the hell. Why would I be humming the Wallykazam theme song here? The one damn place I can listen to my music. DAMMIT!

Eventually, you come to possess in-depth knowledge of the programs that have been forced into your brain in a clockwork orange fashion brainwashing. But at some point the two hour nights of sleep turn to three hour nights then to four and perhaps as much as five. I don't know yet. We're still hovering around four, but I don't want to give up hope that this might grow. As you regain and reclaim your humanity and your bodily function returns to a place of stasis you can acclimate to your new world fully. Once this occurs the wine on a Saturday night comes back, some grown-up shows start appearing in the Netflix recommendations, and before you know it, you're a grown-up, and a parent and you can think again.

As a result, seemingly without any prompting, you turn your long dormant critical and analytical brain toward this world that consumed you for so long. You have questions about what it is you've become an expert in — television for babies and toddlers.

The following are my questions as it relates to the programs on Nick Jr., a favorite in our house.

MAX & RUBY

Where in the hell are your parents?
I asked this question on Facebook and got more responses then I have for anything I've ever posted. Ever!

Also, what is the message that is being sent? Why do you take the forever observant, thoughtful and prepared, if a bit bossy (though keep in mind, by all accounts she's a little girl bunny left to raise her brother, parentless) Ruby and have her always lose in the end to the ever defiant, never attentive, positively dangerous Max, who seems to have the Midas touch?

BLAZE AND THE MONSTER MACHINES

You named yourself, 'Blaze.' The reference is lost on NO ONE. How in god's name did you get the theme song, which repeatedly punctuates the heroic actions of anthropomorphic monster trucks, passed the suits at your company with the refrain of, 'Let's Blaze!'?

PAW PATROL

What kind of municipal budget must you have to have a single outfit for community service providing all manner of emergency first response entirely staffed by dogs? I realize this is totally missing the point and a question that couldn't be asked by the target audience, but these are the things one thinks at some point. This is my life, and these are my thoughts. Seriously.

PEPPA PIG

What the hell is the deal with the constant fat shaming of Daddy Pig? I should note that it's possible this is tweaking some of my personal sensitivities as I'm coming to resemble my namesake.

THE FRESH BEAT BAND

I loved you for two episodes. Now you inspire rage. No questions, just a statement.

THE BUBBLE GUPPIES

Why are you so insistent there be no logic, not even internal logic, regarding the physics of your world? On a recent viewing, there was a fire truck. You are under water! Worse, once they got to where they were going, they couldn't figure out how to get up high until they extended the ladder, which a fish than 'climbed' by SWIMMING UPWARDS NEXT TO IT!! I hate you.

OSWALD

You were perfect. A little slice of Zen-like heaven. Where did you go???

(This story is intended purely as a satire, parody, and spoof. We apologize in advance if any of this story offends the creators, owners, or trademark and copyright holders of Nick Jr. or any of the shows mentioned. We really do love your shows, or at least our kids LOVE your shows, and we love that you create shows that they love. We hope that you can appreciate the humor in this commentary.)

LETTER OF FINAL WARNING
MICHELLE TAN

THE PERFECT MOTHER ASSOCIATION
Private and Confidential

Michelle Tan
Manager of Family Affairs
Home Duties Engineer
BA (Toast Making), MA (Wine Drinking), Ph.D. (Sleep Deprivation)

Dear Michelle,

RE: LETTER OF FINAL WARNING

I am writing to you about your dismal performance as a member of the Perfect Mothers Association, in regards to the terms and conditions of your lifetime membership, which you took out when you were three months pregnant with your first child.

You had sought membership immediately when you saw the second line on the home pregnancy test, declaring that you were the perfect candidate for the Perfect Mother Association, agreeing to adhere to the 42, 354 unbreakable parenting rules, more than four years ago.

The Unofficial Guidebook to Surviving Life With Toddlers

Unfortunately, we have received numerous complaints from your two bosses, Male Toddler Boss, (Master Four) and Female Toddler Boss, (Miss Two) during the last four years and recently, of one particular day on May 15th which was the final straw for our two clients.

On 27th April of this year, you met with Master Four and Miss Two, and they advised you of your highly unsatisfactory performance, and that immediate improvement is required if you want to keep your Perfect Mother status.

In particular, you were advised of the following incidents, which occurred all on February 15th:

1) On February 15th, you woke our two clients who were still so obviously sleepy, at an ungodly hour of eight in the morning for a doctor's appointment, which in their opinion, was not a good enough reason. Let's watch Cartoons? Maybe. What about an unboxing video on YouTube? Most definitely. But for a doctor's appointment, that's downright inappropriate.

2) You then did not allow them to have ice cream or donuts for breakfast. You even tried to trick them into believing that a cheese and spinach omelette was actually as "good" as a donut.

3) You then restricted their access to their IPad that morning, forcing them instead to waste their precious time, looking for their shoes… which by the way, isn't that your job to do?

4) You then forced Master Four to put on pants, when all he really wanted was to wear his pajamas.

5) After the doctor's appointment, during lunchtime, you then proceeded to make lunch. The children had expected macaroni and cheese or chicken nuggets, but to their horror, it was a "sandwich" that was not bought from their favorite fast food restaurant.

6) Mister four then asked you for a blue plate, to which you promptly gave him a blue plate, but he then screamed "NO!" in a pure rage because you should have known that he really wanted the purple plate.

7) You then gave Miss Two her allegedly favorite Pink Cup but Miss Two was wearing yellow socks that morning, and anyone in their right mind would know that their cups and socks must match. So you should have known that she actually wanted the yellow plate and really, you should not even have questioned her why she wanted a yellow plate to drink her milk from.

8) You then served an abomination of a lunch, which left both clients "starving" and "hungry" as you traumatized them with your so-called "healthy sandwich." A sandwich, which in no way resembled Chicken Nuggets or Macaroni and Cheese, which they had expected even though you had announced ten minutes earlier that you were making sandwiches for lunch.

9) Miss Two then nearly fainted when she saw a bit of crust on the right side of her bread. You should be familiar with Toddler 101, which states that all bread slices should be duly de-crusted before being presented. Everyone knows that any bits of crust, however slight, renders the sandwich completely inedible and is, in fact, poisonous to any toddler.

10) To add to their further distress, you then had the audacity to fold their sandwiches in half, into a rectangle shape and not as a triangle, thereby, causing further trauma to the said toddlers. It does not matter that the two toddlers had asked for a folded sandwich because a Perfect Mother would know that the term "folded" could mean, "cut in half", "cut in triangles", "cut in circles", "I don't really want a sandwich", "Chicken nuggets", or Macaroni and Cheese, as deemed acceptable by your toddlers.

11) When they were forced to take a bite, they then found out that you had further tricked them by putting ham and avocado and cheese in their sandwich, as you allegedly claim that you have always done so and they have eaten before, without any issue. It is disappointing to know that a mother could have missed the memo, where it states that toddlers can

develop severe psychological allergies to any ingredients suddenly, which can make them "sick" even if they have eaten them countless of time without incident before. It is one of those common toddler ailments, which can come on within twenty-four hours and then disappear; it is commonly known as "Ihatesit-titis."

12) You then proceeded to peel the bananas for the toddlers knowing full well, that it would traumatize them further as they wanted to peel those bananas themselves, then squish and throw them unto the floor and ask for ice cream. Your thoughtlessness astounded them, as they were unable to perform the full repertoire of their tantrum.

13) During the day, you also did not allow them to flush the toilets repeatedly thirty four times in a row.

14) You did not allow them to watch you pee or look at your poop.

15) You made them take a nap when they were not tired at all.

16) You did not allow them to lick deodorant sticks, the dog, other human beings, the shower stall or any other place or person the toddlers deemed reasonable.

17) You did not have cake for tea even though they were the ones who had eaten it all thirty minutes earlier.

18) You did not know the correct words to the songs from their favorite show and did not allow them to watch the same episode five times in a row. Really, what kind of a mother do you call yourself?

19) You forced them both to bed even though they were not tired at all.

20) You did not read their favorite goodnight book twenty times in a row and even had the audacity to ask them to pick another book. You then had the audacity to fall asleep in mid-sentence.

The Unofficial Guidebook to Surviving Life With Toddlers

21) You refused to let the two toddlers any drink of water even though they were dying of thirst after you said it was lights out and night night.

22) You then threatened to evict them both from your bed at 1:30 am and then refused to dance to Hot Potato for them at 2 am.

After taking into consideration the fact that the toddlers like your hugs, kisses, and smiles, they are willing to give you a second chance. You are expected to improve your conduct and continually strive to meet all the toddlers' demands because that's what perfect moms do.

The intent of this final warning is to provide you with an opportunity to address this situation. Your membership may be terminated if your performance does not improve. You are expected to continually update your skills and enroll in a mind-reading course and learn the art of Toddler speak, where toddlers say what they don't mean and mean what they don't say or say what they mean and mean what they say, in any order.

I propose that we meet again on Mother's Day to review your progress. Please let me know if this time is convenient for you. If you wish to respond to this formal warning letter, please do so by replying in writing.

If the situation is not corrected, you will be subject to further disciplinary action up to and including termination of your lifetime membership with the Association. You may have to stop calling yourself a "Perfect Mother."

Yours sincerely,

B.S. St. Sanctimonious
Founder and Lifetime President of the Perfect Mother Association
Mother to three Fur balls and nine hypothetical children.

DADDY WORDS
BRITON UNDERWOOD

"I'm on the toddler workout routine. I run six laps around the house while trying to put pants on my child. I do thirty sippy cup squats three times a day. I finish up by carrying my flailing free weights to bed four times before they actually stay there"~ Punk Rock Papa

"Is 'dammit' a Daddy word?" My son decides to spring on me in aisle seven of our local grocery store.

I can hear the coupon-conscience grandma fainting in canned goods. Mothers in the pasta section upturn their noses as my swear-curious son unleashes the word 'dammit' like some sort of mythical power word with the power to disrupt the very fabric of our universe. The word leaves his mouth, emblazoning itself on me like a scarlet letter. I am left there. Branded. By my favorite child no less.

As I stand dumbfounded in the international foods section I wonder, what the hell I ever did to this child to make him decide to publicly shame me?

At some point in my children's young lives, collusion occurred. Mommy, a certified potty mouth herself, convinced the easily moldable minds of our children to label any and all bad words as 'Daddy words'. As if these were words ONLY said by me. Regardless of how often Mommy says them. And Daddy Words is all-encompassing. It's not just your run of the mill cuss words. It includes the lower-tiered words like 'dumb' or 'stupid'. How dumb is that?

All the stupid bad words in the world.

Hi, my name is Daddy, and I'm a potty mouth.

There we were, in international foods, my son having just dropped a 'dammit' on the fragile shoppers of Aldis. We weren't even supposed to grocery shop today. This was a trip for milk. How we ended up in aisle seven causing an international scene is a mystery to this day. This certainly wasn't the first time either.

For kids who don't ever swear at home, something happens to my angelic children when we go into public. A sudden, burning desire, overwhelming them. This innate need to inventory the words on the Daddy list. Sharing them with judgmental onlookers. Not just those in our aisle, because when speaking bad words it's important to disregard the rules of an indoor voice. You have to enunciate and project across the entire store.

Can I just say, I don't even f-word say the d-word. That's a mommy personal favorite. Now, I don't want to rehash a previous argument over whether a 'Mommy Words' list should be created. The egregious mommy words ship sailed out of port long ago with mommy at the helm. Swearing off into the sunset.

According to her, another naughty word list would have been too confusing on our children's developing minds. Always keen to preserve their precious developing minds. In an effort to create balance, a 'Kid's Words' list was created and filled with words like 'Shucks', and others taken from an episode of Leave It To Beaver.

The Unofficial Guidebook to Surviving Life With Toddlers

My children, their beautiful flipping heads filled with wonder, also tell their friends at school about Daddy Words. I know this because they tell me so. They tell me this stigma extends far beyond this house. Waylon's dad has to deal with it too. So does Brayden's. My son told me Waylon told him his dad says bad words, and he told Waylon I say bad words too, and that me and Waylon's dad can hang out and say our bad words together. Oh, Brayden wants his bad word saying dad to come too. We can form some sort of three bad word slinging amigos.

This shit wasn't in the 'What to Expect' book. Preschool has been pretty tough on Waylon's dad, Brayden's dad and I. I don't think any of us were prepared for our kids to schoolyard bully us into a bad word club. It isn't like an anti-bullying campaign has broached such a subject or created a support group for us naughty word users. No support system, just unfairly classified as potty mouths.

I thought my kid's enrollment in school would be different. I envisioned it as a play area filled with bad influence, street knowledge, and slang. A place to blame any and all bad habits my son may have on his classmates for ruining his fragile little mind. Instead, my son goes all, 'I learned it from watching you!' on me as he organizes a potty-mouthed dad hunt with his swing set bros.

I haven't felt this ostracized since that time my son dropped an f-bomb during morning mass. That was NOT my fault. I don't know where he learned to say "What the F is going on?" like that. At no point in my life can I recollect directing those words at a gospel choir.

Who can forget the time they played me into saying Daddy Words in front of Grandma. That was an experience I hope old age takes from all of us. As my children stood safely behind grandma, grinning ear to ear, my usage of the word 'butt' had gotten me in trouble. I didn't use it as in 'sit on your butt.' but more like 'Hey, stop being a butt.'

"I told you daddy says that word G-ma." One child said too far away to be strangled.

As I stumbled through a confusing explanation of how sticks and stones break bones but people need to chill off the words I say, Grandma glared on.

"We all know words like butt are daddy words." She said as the kids nodded.

I can't catch a fucking break with this Daddy Words thing.

TODDLERS, HAZMAT SUITS, AND THE MOST WONDERFUL TIME OF THE YEAR
CARRIE TINSLEY

"What are the two sweetest words in the stay-at-home mom's vocabulary? Kindergarten registration" ~Carrie on Y'all

In a home full of little people, parents know that nothing is safe, and we can't have nice things until they go off to college. To that end, no bathroom is out of harm's way once potty training commences.

It is a universally acknowledged truth that toddlers are disgusting. Sorry, Jane Austen. Gross toddlers are also a universal truth.

When I "retired" from teaching to become a stay-at-home mom, there was one aspect I hadn't fully considered: the daycare had basically potty-trained our daughter for me, and we just supported their teaching at home. As the newly-crowned CEO of my home and the little people in it, potty training was now my job, and after my perfectly-easy-to-train daughter, I had two little boys just waiting to pee all over our world.

I wasn't a good potty trainer, and my middle guy was a terrible potty trainee. During the day, we both became busy with our to-do lists. Mine included being a full-time mom and sneaking time to write. His included building forts, dumping the entire contents of our playroom into the floor three times per day, creating zip lines for his toys, and finding his sister's paint to decorate the formerly-white stair railings murder-scene red. While he was so busy, he never felt the overwhelming urge to stop what he was doing and attend to his pee and poop situation. I cleaned up a shit-ton (pun intended) of accidents.

When he decided that using the potty wasn't so bad after all, he still made gigantic, disgusting bathroom messes which defy description in polite society. I could never catch him while he was dropping friends off at the pool…he was like a little bathroom-destroying ninja who did his business and used an entire roll of toilet paper to (almost) get poop wiped off every available surface. Sometimes, I would discover another of his trips to the throne and realize that only the nasty bathroom in the Saw movies was grosser than my bathroom after my kid had been in there.

One year, three weeks before Christmas, the potty issue came to a head. (The puns are killing me.) I took our children to school and daycare for six blessed hours of alone time that restored my soul each week. On this day, I went Christmas shopping in the city, ate lunch alone at a café, and never came home during the day. I was exhausted yet invigorated by the ability to enter and exit stores without immediately being dubbed a traveling circus, to shop without my little people hiding in racks of clothes and startling strangers, to eat a piece of chocolate and not have to share…bliss. With packages loaded in my SUV, I headed to the carpool lines and gathered my children.

When we arrived home, my daughter ran upstairs and then immediately yelled down, "Mama, there's water on the floor in the bathroom!" I was still coming down from the euphoria of my day off when I heard splashing. Lots of splashing.

I ran up the surprisingly soggy stairs to find the toilet gushing water onto the floor, and it was immediately apparent why. Nearly an entire roll of toilet paper, cardboard roll and all, had been stuffed into the bowl but hadn't flushed all the way. Because the universe hated me, probably because of my potty mouth when I encountered lunacy in the loo, the stopper in the toilet's tank hadn't fully settled, so water had literally gushed out of this toilet ALL…DAY…LONG.

That morning, my middle son had dropped a deuce, stuffed the toilet, flushed, and ran out to my car to go to school. The upstairs bathroom, which was conveniently configured above our kitchen, had leaked water all over our two-story house.

Water trickled from my kitchen light fixtures, dripped down the carpeted stairs, and soaked our entire second story, much of the downstairs ceiling, and the garage. I was afraid to turn on the lights, fearing an electrical fire if the wires touched the water. Like the men in E.T., a cleaning crew entered our home a few hours later in hazmat suits to clean our unnatural disaster.

I drank in the front yard.

A week of loud fans and sawed away drywall followed. A 747 could've landed in our living room, but I wouldn't have heard it above the roar of the industrial fans that were drying our house twenty-four hours per day in hopes that our home wouldn't be completely ruined by mold from the water damage at Christmas.

Our insurance coverage required us to hire a plumber to inspect the facilities once everything was dry, and a plumber whose butt crack literally showed above his pants (I so wanted to call the cliché police on his ass), checked out the upstairs toilet and pronounced it healthy, though the victim of a perfect plumbing storm. There had been excessive toilet paper, a temporary tank-stopper failure, and no one home to hear the water running.

I wish I could say that the water damage Christmas was the last time my kid had potty troubles, but it wasn't. I like to consider myself a laid-back parent who can roll with the punches, but the sight of hazmat suits in our living room amongst the Christmas tree, the presents, and the stupid Elf on the Shelf…was a little much.

Our home has thankfully recovered without lasting water or mold damage. Our insurance premiums have increased. Our boys still have terrible bathroom aim, but they know how to courtesy flush and do an emergency plunge maneuver if necessary. In short, we survived the toddler potty training years. Barely.

THE TERRIFYING THREES
ADRIENN HUNT

"I almost signed my name as Parent Hunt on a school form in case you're wondering what kind of day I had." ~Adrienn Hunt, Writer

I'm not ashamed to leash my three-year-old when venturing out into busy public places. I'm sure it's not called a leash, but I'm too tired to look it up. That's what toddlers do to you.

Right now, you're either wondering where to get one for your own kid, or you're looking at me like I'm a lunatic which means either you've forgotten what it's like to have a three-year-old or you're still back in the "terrible" twos, lost in the illusion of having everything under control.

You might even be in the trenches of infancy, hooked up to a breast pump wondering why she won't latch on. You are wondering if you make enough milk. Postpartum hormones and Pinterest are fueling your unrealistic expectations while you try to remember how many days it has been since you had your last shower. Don't bother. Everything you own smells like spit up, and you don't have any clean towels anyway.

Maybe you're a newlywed, young and in love. You haven't made it into the trenches at all, but you're planning on it soon, and you read all of the parenting books-fully prepared for what's to come and confident your kids will listen to every word you say because you don't have any yet. Yes, you there, still wearing makeup and matching socks, your hair all clean and neatly pulled up into a tidy, cute bun. I bet your purse is even full of things that belong to you.

I was you once, just like you'll be me one day, standing in the middle of your kitchen asking "How in the hell did you get on top of the fridge?" And…. "Why do you have a marker cap? What do you mean you drew on the Kitty? Why are your hands sticky? Hey, your sleeve is not a napkin. Don't ever smear hair gel on the T.V. again! Why does it smell like poop in here? Who gave you a piece of gum? Why are you crying? Is Kitty in your toy box? What did you stick up your nose? How did you get outside? Where are your pants? Why are you crying? I gave you a mini tootsie roll, how did you get it all over yourself? Why did you change your clothes? You have to wear a coat. I know you can do it yourself, but we don't have time for that. Do you know what grandma used to say to me? I'll give you something to cry about. SHIT is a bad word, don't say it. One! Two! Oh dear god, what do I do if get to three?! Do you have to pee? Stop doing that. Where are you? Don't spit on your tablet. Did you just feed your baby sister a booger? How did you get all wet? Leave the cat alone. Get down from there. Just tell me why you are crying! Don't put your finger in my mouth. Where is your sucker? What do you mean you wiped your butt?"

It won't just happen at home either, and that's when things get tricky because calling your toddler an A-hole in public is not as widely accepted as it probably should be.

Teaching young children how to behave in a restaurant has to be done in a restaurant which is awkward when your toddler asks the woman in the booth behind you why she's so fat. And while I'm thinking about it, is it really necessary to have a constant supply of sugar packets at every table? Don't worry, Karen, you'll get a big tip to clean up this mess. And also, you're out of sugar packets at this table because my kid shoved them all down into her drink cup after she pried the lid off with her freakishly strong fingers.

Taking a potty-training toddler out to eat means never eating hot food ever again. (I said that as if I even know what hot food tastes like anymore. I mean, I could be served dinner in Hell on a metal platter, and it would still be cold) Because even if they don't have to go potty, they are fascinated by the fact that every restaurant has a bathroom, like all this time it was some big secret, and they will need to see EVERY SINGLE ONE...

Then they insist on washing their hands ALL BY THEMSELVES, except they can't reach the soap which pisses them off. So there you are trying to reason with your little A-hole about how sorry you are that they can't reach the soap, but someday they will be big and be able to reach it all by themselves. Which causes them to start yelling things like, "I DON'T WANT TO GET BIG!" until a lady rips a fart while peeing and suddenly your kid couldn't care less about soap but wants to know "Who farted mommy?" and "Why does it smell so bad in here?"

Shopping is not as fun as it used to be either. You attempt to try on clothes in the fitting room and as soon as your pants come off your kid takes off crawling under the wall into someone else's fitting room. So you profusely apologize and blindly flail an arm under the wall hoping to connect with your kid's leg or arm or hair-really anything at this point. Embarrassed, you apologize again and again to the mystery lady shopper in the fitting room next to yours.

Before you know it, your kid runs off to play hide and seek with you in the clothes racks. It's cute and funny for about .03 seconds, but after ten minutes go by and you still can't find her or hear giggling anymore, you start to think someone might have grabbed her up. You panic. Strangers start asking you what your child was wearing, and you feel like a terrible mother because you don't even know what your child is wearing. A store clerk asks you to calm down and stay in one spot. The loudspeakers are chanting "CODE RED," The whole store goes into lockdown, and no one is allowed to come in or out and all the sudden you can't breathe.

Then you realize a nice woman is softly telling you that she thinks she found your kid hiding right over there. So you run to there, and there she is, and you're crying and she's crying because you're crying and you leave without buying anything and later that night while you're giving her a bath you'll ask "Why didn't you come out from hiding behind the clothes at the store? Did you hear mommy and all the strangers calling for you?"

"Yes. I heard you calling and calling and calling, and I just was laughing very quietly."

So, yeah. I'm not ashamed of leashing my three-year-old.

IF ONLY OUR MAMA'S TOLD US THERE'D "PEE" DAYS LIKE THIS

HOLLY RUST

> "You know you're a boy mom when... You yell "Get your hands out of your pants" ALL DAY LONG! ~Hollydays Chicago

I never considered myself a girly-girl. Growing up, I liked fashion and make-up, but I also liked to catch grasshoppers, play sports, learn about cars, wear sneakers and follow my older brothers around. Most would have classified me a tomboy.

When I got married and my husband and I started considering a family, I immediately knew I wanted boys. Girls are amazing too, don't get me wrong, but I felt like I was much better suited to be a boy mom. Well, the universe obliged and gave me two beautiful boys. It was instant love at first sight when my first son arrived. He stared into my eyes, held my finger and filled my heart with immeasurable pride and love. In my imagination, I pictured us going on grand adventures, playing catch, cheering on the Cubs, catching bugs together, and him always loving his momma. Of course, all of those things do happen, but what I wasn't expecting––was to be engrossed in all things gross. No one warned me. No one told me about the gross. A heads up would have been nice.

What do I mean by gross?

If you have a toddler boy, you may know what I mean. If not, let me enlighten you with a few examples of what it's like a day in the life of a boy mom.

When my son was an infant, the minute his diaper came off, there was a geyser of pee coming out of his little body. It was quite impressive. The fluids decorated the walls, soaked his clothes (and mine), got in my hair, and sometimes even targeted his face. I know…. Vomit. I may have even gotten it in my mouth a little a few times when first experiencing this. I learned quickly to use another diaper to shield myself from his pee-wrath during diaper changes.

As someone who used to get grossed out fairly easy, I'm not sure how I made it through those days. Constantly sporting bodily fluids of another human all over your clothes... is so not cute.

Fast forward a few years and now I get the pleasure of cleaning up urine off the walls, floors, and toilets in all of my bathrooms. Even though I shout, "IN THE TOILET" multiple times a day, the boys take that as a suggestion rather than the rule. I like to refer to the clean up as "Peeapalooza time." My boys think it's funny. I do not.

Quick pro-parenting tip (just kidding, I'm not a pro but have learned the hard way): Don't dare not walk in and interrupt them mid-stream because if they turn, the stream follows. I warned you.

My son and I do like to explore as I had always envisioned, but some of that exploration consists of him digging in his nose to show me his proud discoveries. If I'm lucky, he won't wipe his findings on me, but rather the couch or his wall at night while in bed. He's made quite the masterpiece of wall art before. You'd be impressed.

After long days of running around and playing outside, he's most excited to come home, remove his shoes, and insist I smell his feet. Since I'm his mom and I love him so, I always appease him. By now, all the hairs in my nose have burned off from the boy smells anyway. I'm unsure as to why the smell of his feet could wake a hibernating bear––maybe it's time to re-evaluate what I feed him? Or change out his shoes every few weeks? Either way, the shoes have made their home in the garage where they will stay until I burn them.

At least once a day I get called a poopy head. All out of love, of course. He also giggles with pride each time he lets one rip. He's the master at "hot boxing." I no longer cringe when he yells for me to wipe his butt while I'm having a glass of wine with a neighbor. Plus, let's be honest, better I do it then for him to do it and then give the whole house pink eye. Am I right? That's no fun. He also likes to blow his nose and show me what's inside the tissue. "Ewwwwwww, look at this Mommy!" For some reason, it's always when we are at a restaurant too.

I'll admit, between my boys and my husband, there are days I can't take it. I beg to be in a fart-free zone or respectfully ask that their fingers stay out of their noses and away from me. I'll yell, "CLOSE THE DOOR," so I don't have to hear them do their thing while sitting on the porcelain God. I sometimes even pay a cleaning service to tackle the boy infested bathrooms... because I just can't.

You can also only handle saying, "get your hands out of your pants please," so many times a day. By the way, what exactly is the fascination with boys (and husbands) touching their bits twenty-four seven? Is it cold? Is it falling off? Do you need to make sure it's still there? It is, I promise. When I tell them this, I get a smirk and a response that it itches. In which case, I march them straight to the bath. Maybe if they wash the itches off, I won't have to see them playing with it all the time you'd think.

When we do play dates, I usually like to hang with other boy moms, so they don't judge. When our boys do something cringe-worthy, we hug in solidarity. We get it. We know what's up. It's not us. It's them. It's the way it is. We weren't ready for it, but now we own it. We are boy moms. We love them in all their boy glory regardless.

At one play date, my girlfriend invited us over to go swimming. Meaning we sat poolside chatting and the boys played in the water. About an hour into the play date, my older son ran to the side of the deck and pulled his swim trunks down to pee on a wooden post.

That's right, like an animal.

Or, like a boy that was seemingly raised in a barn. A boy that didn't remember the manners I've been teaching him throughout his four short years of life. As the words, "OMG, noooooooooooooooo…." were coming out of my mouth… he opened stream. I was prepared to pay for her to have a new deck, apologize profusely, and accept that we would never be invited over to play or swim again. As my face turned bright red with utter embarrassment, she told me her son does it all the time and she truly doesn't care. "Better out here than run through the house wet." She continued, "and who wants to get up to help take off his wet shorts anyway?!" She poured me a glass of white wine and raised her glass to cheers. "Here's to boy moms!"

It was at that moment; I knew it wasn't just me. I knew I was a good mom. Being a mom has been the greatest gift I've ever known. I'll take the pee, boogers, farts, and hands in pants if it means I'm their favorite girl. If it means, they'll let me cuddle with them into their teens. If it means they'll let me explore with them forever. I've accepted the gross. I even learned to laugh and dare I say love the gross.

When you become a mom you'll be thrown into a world of unknowns, but all the urine and poop in the world wouldn't stop you from doing it all over again. Cheers to the boy moms, but now I think it's time for a girls trip.

A DAY IN THE LIFE OF A TODDLER
LYNDEE BROWN

"My parenting style is mostly me running around in circles pretending I know what is going on." ~#Lifewithboys

I wake up to the sound of a crashing baby gate on the monitor. It takes me a moment to register that I am awake and the sound is real. I book it downstairs in record time to see my son has made it up the kitchen counter and is squatting on top of the refrigerator. I croon to him softly, "Mommy is here and I will help you down, stay right where you are." My heart is beating wildly. I thankfully get to him before he decides to do something toddler-ish like jump. I hug him to me and he yells, "No nuts!" What?! Ah, crap, what has he heard on TV or from his older brother or father? He pumps his fists wildly and squirms. I set him down and he throws himself on the ground, rolling around and wailing, "Nooo nutssssss!"

At this point I am looking around trying to figure out the mystery of the "no nuts" and I have no clue beyond the obvious meaning and he is too young to understand that, so I am lost. The six-year-old walks in and clears the sleep from his eye and huffs, "Mom he wants donuts". Thank God siblings speak the language of the toddler otherwise, I would be so screwed. I walk back over to the fridge and sure enough, shoved to the back is yesterday's box of donuts someone thought they were able to hide from the all-knowing toddler. I grab the box, set it on the table and allow the boys to take a donut after I lecture that they have to ask for them first and climbing is not safe, yadda, yadda, yadda…. I need a vat of coffee and a giant no-nut.

I would have a coffee, but I am out of milk, creamer, and everything because I tried to wait until I was child free to go to the grocery store. I laugh at myself for thinking the words, child-free and store and put on my big girl pants and loaded everyone up. I drop the six-year-old off at school and we are on our way. After I detangle my child from the parent proof harness toddler seat and bribe him into the buckled part of the grocery cart, we begin our shopping adventure. It starts out fine for the first five minutes, then he starts reaching and knocking down boxes as we go down the aisle. After a lecture and more bribery, we make it to the part of the store that has things like toothpaste, but they are across from the toy aisle. Stupid retail store layout people. My son whips his head to the side and shouts, "Fuck, big fuck!" The elderly lady looks at me horrified as I am hiding my silent laughing face behind a box of cereal. "Trrr, truck", I correct. He points and says, "Fuck" again. We go and get him a big truck while the judgmental lady remains aghast.

We head to a playdate at my friend's house after lunch, which we are both mostly wearing thanks to my son's mad throwing skills. Thank goodness she has a toddler too or I would have had to go home and change and look somewhat put together. I walk in and she puts the boys in the living room with all the toys where we can watch them and she hands me a coffee. I give her the mom nod of appreciation and we drink in absolute silence for a second until the toddler battle for a single toy leads to a tantrum and an epic meltdown.

We get them to settle with a snack and some always dependable Blue's Clues. The boys are engrossed in the show. She wants to show me something concerning in her yard. We step out on the porch for a second and come back in and the living room is vacant and we hear giggles. The boys had found the sharpie markers in another room and ran down the hallway without the lid on. It was mostly my child, he loves art of any kind. My friend's house is not only a home, but it is also a studio that she has to have clients come through. She is horrified and shrieking about her walls. I was her a few months back before my toddler broke me. I use to freak out about keeping things nice. I have accepted that my house is going to have unexplained wall art, broken decorations and gross furniture until they are older. My toddler had already trained me. I felt bad though because it wasn't my house and apologized and went and tried all the google tricks for permanent marker removal. Finally, I ended up running to the home improvement store for matching paint and a paintbrush. We fixed the walls and I gave her a hug and told her all the playdates can be at my house.

On our way home I can tell my son is extremely tired and fighting sleep. The boy needs a serious nap. I try to get him to settle in with his blanket and a stuffed animal which he immediately throws on the floor. I imagine if one had to wrangle a spider monkey, that is what it probably looks like I am doing every time I try to get my pissed off toddler in his five-point harness. After five attempts I am successful in getting him buckled safely and sweating like I just got done working out.

I roll down the windows half way and turn up the music slightly to drown out the angry howls. The howls stop and I look in the review mirror right into his defiant little eyes. Then he throws his shoes out the window, while we are on the interstate in the middle lane. I rolled up the windows and put the child safety lock on and pretended nothing happened. Sometimes it is better if you don't react, I remind myself. I cannot believe he threw thirty dollars out the window and he doesn't know how hard it is to find decent shoes to fit his weirdly fat and wide toddler feet.

I look back and he is finally asleep. I pull up to my house and keep the car running. I make the executive decision to not take the terrifying toddler out of the seat. I stay in the car and stay productive by paying all of my bills and call my Mom to vent. I tell her my day so far, while she laughs hysterically at me. She tells me it is karma from when I was a toddler. Forty-five minutes later he wakes up and off we go again.

I swear he knew I was at the end of my rope because the rest of the day he was a saint and cute as a button. He gave kisses and snuggles. He said sweet things like, "Love Mommy!" He even fell asleep on my shoulder with all the toddler trust he could give. I laid him down on his bed and he looked like a sleeping angel. I watched him sleep and tried to remind myself that I needed to enjoy him now, the crazy and the sweet because someday he would become a tween.

FOR WHOM THE SMELL TOLLS
RENEE ROBBINS

"I miss toddlerhood. We don't get nearly as excited around here when someone poops in the potty." ~This is My Day Job

What is it about little boys and bad smells?

Now that my son is thirteen, his obsession with how he smells has become less about making himself the target of intense hatred of anyone who rides in a car with him, and more about smelling…well, better. I suspect there is a girl in the picture. I just spent twenty minutes in the body spray aisle with him, testing scents like "The Dark Lord of Disco" and "Manscape Inferno" (I may have made those up) at his request. So yeah – there's a girl.

Meanwhile, I have to smell like every middle-aged used car salesman from the seventies in the hopes that, with my wisdom and guidance, he will figure out the meaning of "sparingly." While I am optimistic about his new maturity, I also hope that he knows where to spray it.

Whenever he left the bathroom when he was little, I'd exclaim "Phew! Now we have to buy a new house!" And he'd giggle, even though he sometimes looked worried. And I'd spray. I used an "all-natural" citrus-scented, non-aerosol spray because Lysol makes me gag, and who doesn't like oranges? It became part of my prime directive of raising a boy with enough self-awareness to complete the Parenting FTW trifecta of putting the seat down, washing his hands, and spritzing the bathroom before vacating the premises. I was clearly on track for Mother of the Year. I pre-qualified myself for bonus mother-in-law points down the road – in my head, my son's future mate was already thanking me for instilling good habits.

Until that day. That fateful day that I got distracted by his sister and her standard refusal to wear pants. It is amazing how many different shapes a toddler can twist themselves into in an effort to stay naked.

"Momma! I fix it!" he said as he emerged from the master bathroom. I looked up from the writhing, squealing mass of limbs I was trying to compress into duck pajamas, complete with happy yellow duck feet, and smiled encouragingly. I watched him strut across the room like a tiny little Prince of Poo.

"Yaaaaaaay! What did you fix?"

"I not stinky anymore!"

"Good for you, sweetie! So proud of you!"

Something about the way he kept smiling gave me pause.

"….and how did you do that, honey?"

"I spray it on me!"

I don't remember now, where I got the citrus air freshener. Who knows? It contained, not surprisingly, citrus oil. It was 'ALL NATURAL!" So, he'd walk around smelling like a giant orange. That was ok with me. Probably.

I stared at him for a beat or two. "Where did you spray it?"

He pointed down, kind of sly like he was letting me in on a secret. More giggles.

"Did you spray it...ON you? On your privates?"

Enthusiastic nod.

Oil: A substance that permeates. Citrus: a substance that burns. Don't believe me? Drink some OJ next time you bite your tongue. My sweet little boy had just sprayed the essential oil equivalent of Agent Orange on Amos, Andy, and the boys. I could tell that the concern that was creeping into my happy Mommy smile was starting to worry him – that he thought he might be in trouble. In those situations, experts will tell you to be careful not to overreact, because you might scare your child. But I didn't have time for that calm, rational mommy bullshit right now. I figured I had less than a minute.

Thirty seconds later he was sitting in a tub that was filling with cool water.

Thirty-five seconds later, I was nearly airborne on the way downstairs to the kitchen.

It was then, as I rounded the landing that he started to scream.
Not "mad cause I have to take a bath," scream. SCREAM.

The warnings on the bottle said to flush the affected area with cold water. Done. Somewhere in the back of my mind, I believed I had read that whole milk will soothe burns like this better than water, so I grabbed it, and some yogurt for good measure, which seems ridiculous in retrospect. His screams were louder now, and while the situation would hold some humor for me later, that sound will cut any mother to the quick, especially when she is not completely sure of her game plan. I was fighting back silly, unhelpful tears.

My daughter met me in the hall, alarmed by the commotion. Wearing one leg of duck pajamas with the other trailing hopefully behind her, she began following me, plaintively and earnestly repeating, "Mama? Feff? Mama? Bruvver?"

"Yes, baby, Seth is hurt. He will be okay. Can you wait here with your bears?" She assured me that she could not. But I didn't have time to soothe her, either, because my little boy was falling apart.

I made him sit as I poured cold milk all over his business, which horrified him further because he really liked milk and now the bottle was empty. His screams of pain were replaced by wails of confusion – it seemed he thought that having milk dumped on him was some sort of punishment. Because apparently, in this family we subscribe to the slapstick theory of child discipline. "What have you done? THAT'S IT! A MILK BATH FOR YOU! Did you just roll your eyes at me? DON'T MAKE ME OPEN THIS GO-GURT, MISTER!"

"TAKE ME TO HOSPITAAAAAAALLLLLLL!" my little boy wailed, and I know what you are thinking, Judgy McJudgeface – why didn't I take him to the hospital? Because I had to stop the burning first. Throwing him, naked and screaming with loins of fire in the back of a car with a half-naked duck-footed toddler and driving to the ER in the middle of winter to have them put him in a $20,000 bath of cold water and give him a $400 ibuprofen seemed sort of….stupid, at the time.

Meanwhile, my daughter had decided that her brother was going to die. I could tell by the way she kept keening "BRUVVER DYIIIIINGGGGG HELLLP HIIIIMMMUHHHH!"

They were pointing at each other and howling, one naked in a bathtub full of milk and water and the other wilted to the ground from the sheer weight of humanity. As is customary, it was then that she began the Sacred Toddler Ululation stage of grief, mournfully waving her arm over her head in a Mockingjay-ish salute and farewell to her confused brother. May the odds be ever in your favor. Even her duck feet looked distraught.

My husband called, as I googled "choosing a therapist for your toddler."

"WHO SPRAYS AIR FRESHENER ON THEIR OWN BUTT??" I answered.

"What? What is going on?"

"Nothing. Tell you later."

Google search confirmed that I am the worst mother in the world.

No, it actually said that.

Once I had rinsed all the dairy product off my child, the next step was to coat the area in vegetable oil which, while counterintuitive, will stop the absorption. I even found a suggestion for making a flour paste. The similarity to my Aunt Ava's Church Picnic Fried Chicken recipe was not lost on me, but the eleven herbs and spices seemed like overkill.

Within an hour or so, the crisis was over. The redness was gone, everyone had stopped screaming, and I had replaced the milk.
I had also thrown away the air freshener. As I watched him test the body spray today, I couldn't help but remember. He remembers, too, but since he's a teen now, he doesn't like to talk about it.

And now and then, my daughter will say "Remember when Seth sprayed air freshener on his butt?"

The therapist says that's normal.

MUFFIN WARS
ANDREW KNOTT

"I see that you're waiting for my parking spot, but we'll probably be sitting here for at least twenty minutes because my toddler just learned to buckle her own seat belt" ~ Explorations of Ambiguity

I peeled the brown paper wrapping down from the sides of an oversized chocolate chip muffin and placed it on the silver metal table in front of my almost two-year-old daughter. She had just scrambled up on the stool attached to the table outside the gas station convenience store. It was shortly after nine o'clock on a Tuesday morning and she was practically licking her lips in anticipation of the breakfast feast in front of her.

Perhaps what amounts to a giant cupcake isn't the most nutritious breakfast for a toddler (or anyone, really). However, it was a special occasion, so when she spotted the treat in the Wawa display case while I was getting coffee, I didn't put up a fight. We had just dropped my middle child, age three, off at preschool on his second day and, for the first time, it was just the two of us out on the town. So yeah, I really just wanted to share the muffin. I needed sugar to cheer me up.

Olivia dove into the meal head first. Literally. Instead of reaching for the muffin, she placed her hands on the table and leaned her head down to take a huge bite, like a pie eating contest participant. Slightly horrified, I swooped in and tore a small piece off the muffin top before she could ruin the whole thing with her slobber. My interruption was not well received. She squealed a "No!" and gesticulated wildly in my direction. I offered her the piece I had torn off in an attempt to quell the screeching, but she swatted my hand away like a basketball player rejecting an opponent's shot attempt.

We repeated this dance several times before I realized what was going on. There could be no cooperation in this muffin eating affair because this was war. If I wanted any pieces of chocolate-studded heaven to pair with my coffee, I would have to fight dirty. When you have a toddler, you better become comfortable with guerilla warfare sooner rather than later if you want to survive. Because I am a stay-at-home parent and Olivia is my third child, I was more than ready to fight fire with fire. I wasn't about to let a snot-nosed toddler, no matter how adorable, stand in the way of my well-earned breakfast treat.

I had just dropped my little boy off at school and cried in the car all the way to the gas station. The little boy who has practically been an extension of my body since he was born. The one I still fall asleep holding most nights in our favorite rocking chair. The one that, when he wakes up in the middle of the night, every night, only wants me. Yes, that one. I had just dropped him off with strangers and he had teared up when I turned to walk away. Dammit, I deserved a muffin!

Luckily, over the years I have developed a couple of tricks for stealing food from toddlers. Well, mainly one trick. And it isn't particularly tricky, it's kind of just a thing I do. Whatever. It was time to employ my masterful strategy.

I pretended that I didn't understand that she didn't want me to touch her food. I kept pulling off larger and larger pieces. Each time, she protested vehemently.

"Oh," I mumbled with muffin crumbs stumbling out of my mouth, "you didn't want me to take anymore? I thought you did. My mistake."

She didn't seem to understand or believe my explanation and, judging by the timbre of her squeals and the rising color in her cheeks, she seemed to be getting angrier and angrier. Fortunately, her anger only opened the door for me to steal more muffin. Toddlers can be so irrational sometimes.

Now, I know this tactic seems mean, but hear me out. I really wanted to eat that muffin.

In addition, Olivia is no angel when it comes to respecting other people's food. Just ask her older brothers. She torments them endlessly at dinner time. During the day, she is your average toddler: adorable, volatile, short-limbed, relatively uncoordinated. However, as dinner time approaches, she transforms into an octopus.

When the plates of food are set down on the dinner table, she moves from chair to chair and place setting to place setting via jet propulsion, draping one tentacle over her brother's shoulder from behind to distract so she can sweep the other tentacle around in front to suck up some chicken nuggets. Before the boys can even enunciate their screams for help, she has already moved on to the next plate and the next victim.

Her brothers quickly become frustrated and frightened because they are inexperienced and weak. They lack the street smarts and cold-bloodedness to deal effectively with a kleptomaniacal toddler-octopus hybrid.

So, you see, don't feel bad for Olivia. She's usually the one dishing it out. Or, rather, filching from other people's dishes.

A few days after the muffin incident, I found myself again seated across the table from my pint-sized nemesis. We were home alone and still trying to find ways to pass the time. Not surprisingly, we had settled on eating. This time, we were dining at the tiny picnic table on our back porch. I was sitting sideways because my legs wouldn't fit under the table without my knees touching my ears. Olivia was picking at wedges from a mandarin orange that were piled in a small plastic yellow bowl. She had peeled it herself. She was getting good at that. It only took her about seventeen minutes this time.

She seemed weirdly agreeable. She even started handing me pieces of orange, pointing at my mouth, and saying "Mommy," which is what she calls me and pretty much everyone else. This was so fun! Quality time with my little girl!

Then, suddenly, it turned.

After I ate the second of her offerings, she grimaced, popped up from her seat, marched around the edge of the table, and planted herself firmly in front of me.

"Mine!" she said, pointing her chubby little finger in my face.

She thrust her upturned hand out toward me, ready to collect.

I gave her a confused and slightly terrified look.

She glared at me with her arctic blue eyes. Her dirty blonde bangs were pulled up in a messy water spout hair-do, which made her look slightly ridiculous and weirdly intimidating. With that kind of hairstyle, she clearly had nothing to lose.

Dread overcame me as I slowly realized I had walked straight into an ambush.

"Um," I mumbled, searching for a way out. "I ate it. I can't give it back."

She squealed a squeal that can only be described as bloodthirsty.

Then her hand shot forward, grabbed my shirt collar with a fierce grip, and pulled me to my feet.

The next thing I knew, I was being dragged by my shirt, hunched over because the person doing the dragging was less than three feet tall, out into the sunny backyard by my lone remaining daytime companion and chief tormentor.

She set me free just long enough so she could slam the rickety screen door behind us. I considered making a break for it, but I knew it was hopeless. There was no escape. I decided to stand and take my dressing down like a man/mommy.

Boy, was I in for it. She clearly remembered the muffin.

HELL HATH NO FURY LIKE A TODDLER WHO DIDN'T GET HER PONY TOOTHBRUSH

SHERRY WHITE

> *"Kids should be in charge of naming things because life would be a lot funnier. For instance, my three-year-old just referred to diarrhea as poopy throw-up."* ~The Messy Christian

I remember talking with a friend after she had just been through a horrible tantrum with her son at the store. In her frustration, she commented on how she felt it was only her kid that acted that way because she never sees anyone else's kid do that. I told her that this couldn't be farther from the truth. That she just wasn't witnessing it. But trust me… it happens to all of us, especially when your child has set up residence in the kingdom of Toddlerdom.

It's so easy for us moms to think our children are the only ones that throw epic tantrums at the store. They are not. EVERY kid does it. EVERY kid. Even the ones that walk into the store and hold their mommy's hand and don't beg for candy at the checkout. They have done it too, but you just weren't there to see it. And if there are any grandmas out there who say that their kids never acted like that, they're lying. (This is a shout out to my mom who swears we never acted like that yet at the same time tells me my daughter acts just like me.) It's not intentional. I just think their memory of these events has faded over time, which should give us all hope!

My daughter is very sweet. She's downright precious. And I have had several people tell me how well behaved she is and how happy she is, and they are right. But she is not always that way. She saves those moments for when it's just me, her, and a couple of hundred pairs of eyes at Walmart. She has thrown some pretty epic tantrums, and this story is only one of many.

It all started when I so graciously offered to buy her a battery-operated, spinning toothbrush. I was replacing her brothers, and she wanted one just like him. It was to be her very first spinning toothbrush. She picked out the pony one. That wasn't much of a surprise because it had been the year of the pony for her — everything pony. As we entered the checkout lane, she ever so politely asked if she could place it on top of the conveyor belt (this is code for she cried and whaled at a high pitch until I could decipher what she was talking about). I bent down and told her if she stopped crying immediately that I would allow her to put it on the conveyor belt. She did, and so I let her do it. But when all the bags had been placed in the cart, and we were leaving the aisle, she began her intense screaming campaign for the toothbrush.

Now, sometimes I can tell by the way she is crying if she is capable of being reasoned with and other times she is too far gone in her rampage to even think of trying to calm her down. I was dealing with the latter. But because I am a very hopeful person, I tried to explain that if she would stop screaming, she could have the toothbrush once we got to the car. But needless to say, she didn't care. So I quickly picked her up. But trying to maneuver a cart, while your toddler is acting like a spinning toothbrush herself is difficult, so I placed her in the back of the cart.

In her fury, she began opening bags and throwing out the ones that didn't contain the toothbrush. She did it with the skill of an expert baton twirler. This is what led to me running over the bags with my own cart.

Let me repeat that. I WAS RUNNING OVER THE BAGS WITH MY OWN CART!

All the while, she was screaming like a banshee. I'm pretty sure there were some young twenty-somethings in the checkout lanes vowing never to reproduce upon seeing such a sight.

As I picked the bags up and placed them back into the cart, she had found the bag containing the toothbrush. But too bad for her and everyone at Walmart, I was not going to let that happen after the way she had just acted. So I clutched the bag with one hand and drove the cart with the other. It was a battle of wills, and I felt like Rocky Balboa determined to stay in the ring. I'm pretty sure "Eye of the Tiger" began playing in the background.

Meanwhile, I had to keep glancing back to make sure my five-year-old was still in tow. My daughter, still screaming like a wounded Mariah Carey, began smacking my hands, spitting mad that she couldn't have in her possession the very rare and valuable pony toothbrush. I won't go into detail describing the events that took place once we reached the car, but I will tell you that she did not get that toothbrush for a week!

After wrestling her into the car seat and feeling like I had just gone ten rounds with Mike Tyson, I settled into the front seat of the car with a deep sigh. If only my friend could have seen me. She would know that she is not alone. Not at all.

PINT SIZE POLITICIAN
SARAH HONEY

"If you give a kid a Band-Aid, chances are he will need another and another and another!" ~ Thank You Honey

The black Little Tikes Cozy Truck stood parked on the sidewalk in front of the garage. The sun was shining as the thin layer of morning dew evaporated into the air. The front driver side door was open of the Little Tikes Truck, and the little trunk was open and hanging down.

Little Dude was busy, and he had that determinate look on his face. The facial expression that meant he was going to do it by himself, no matter how difficult the task. He was deep in thought. As he walked back and forth through the garage studying all of his toys and other items we had stored on the shelves in the garage.

Every single step Little Dude took was well maneuvered and calculated. Little Dude would stop every so often and carefully look at an object. As he reached down to pick it up, his facial expression changed from that determined look to a great big smile. He then carried the item back to where his Little Tikes Truck was parked. Little Dude placed it ever so meticulously into his Little Tikes Trunk adjusting the other objects to make room for the new object to fit so perfectly.

After his fourth trip of pacing through the garage and loading his Little Tikes Truck with his new found treasures, he closed the trunk and the driver side door. "There, I am done," declared Little Dude. Little Dude walked over and kissed me. He then said, "Bye mommy, I am all packed" in that sweet baby voice. I kissed and hugged him back and said, "Bye baby, where are you going"?

"Oh, don't worry momma, I am going to Papa's house," Little Dude said. "Okay, drive safely," I said. He got into his Little Tikes Truck and drove off. Little Dude headed down the driveway and turned onto the sidewalk. He turned back and waved. Moments later he stops and then said, "Hey mommy, can you drive me instead. Papa lives too far, and my feet are tired," Little Dude said.

When I told Little Dude, we would have to plan a weekend to go to Papa's house because he lives five hours away. Little Dude would not have it. There was no falling to the ground tantrum. There was just an award-winning argument with factual well thought out details as to why we needed to go immediately to Papa's house. He listed what he was going to do with every item he put in his Little Tikes Truck. Little Dude was determined and strong-willed and had a comeback for every reason I gave to why we could not go right then and there. This little three- year- old was smart, quick, and it was scary.

The determined characteristic that Little Dude possesses has followed him through his little life. The first warm day in April, after what seemed like the longest winter ever. We were shopping at Target. As we strolled down the aisles, Little Dude sat happily in the cart. He said, "Hello" and waved at every person that walked by. Little Dude would tell people about his day and asks others questions about their day whether they wanted to know or not.

At check out, Little Dude said, "hello" to the cashier, then he said, "Do you want to come over to my house for a playdate." He said it so casually just like he would talk to one of his friends at preschool. My mouth just about fell on the floor as I nervously laughed. The beautiful blond girl cashier looked to be about college age. She smiled and responded to him quickly, "Thanks, buddy, but I have to finish working and checking people out." He said, "Maybe another time then." The lady behind us in line started laughing and gave me those judgmental eyes that said, "What are you teaching your son." My face turned as red as the Target Balls outside the entrance of the store. I felt utterly mortified and embarrassed. I gathered my bags, and we strolled out of the store. I could not believe my child just tried to pick up a college girl from Target.

Little Dude was determined to make friends with everyone in the community from the youngest members to the oldest members, as well as the local businesses. He loved to visit the fire station and a realtor's office next door to Starbucks because they had a fish tank and a giant goldfish they called Nemo. Every time we were in town we had to stop in. The women at the front desk knew him by name, and she would always give him a lollipop. Little Dude loved enlisting the other parents at the playground to "watch" him do whatever he was doing. "Watch this" then he would question them, "Did you just see me do that."

One day Little Dude and I went out to a cafe in town for lunch. While we were waiting for our meal, he began talking to the businessmen sitting at the table next to us. As we were eating lunch, a cute blond girl sat down at the on the other side of us. In between bites of peanut butter and grape jelly and crunching on BBQ chips, Little Dude struck up a conversation with the cute blond girl. "You should try my peanut butter and grape jelly sandwich, it's my favorite," he said. The girl was sweet and talked with him.

Little Dude may have a case of "attention loving." I do not think that's the case. He's just a little boy with a big heart who is very determined and wants to include everyone in everything he does. He's a spirit lifter, a happiness seeker, a humorist, and a person that when he finds something enjoyable. He wants everyone to participate and be a part of it. Even people he doesn't know.

Picking Little Dude up from preschool was always an entertaining event. I never knew what his teacher was going to say about his day or if she was going to lecture me about how to parent or suggest book titles. Little Dude's teacher would tell me how Little Dude was the classroom representative. That he felt it was his duty to "represent his friends" and argued on his friend's behalf, why they should not be in trouble. Little Dude would advocate for the entire class by making a strong case that the whole class needed to have a second serving of the chocolate chip cookies.

Some people call Little Dude's personality friendly or obnoxious. I call it ingenious. That invite for a "play date" could just be his code for, or his way of saying, "Do I have your vote in 2050" and "can I count on your support." Talking to the community members at Target, or in town may just be his way to sell his campaign mission. Taking a firm stance for Mac & Cheese to be its own food group and ice cream to be served for dessert after every meal no matter the season. Petitioning to raise bedtimes for children around the United States. Little Dude would unite children around the world by having parades and fireworks as part of every day! Vote for Little Dude for President!

MOTHER AND DAUGHTER TALKS
BIANCA JAMOTTE LEROUX

*"Every day I lose my mind and my keys.
I know my keys will show eventually…"
~ Bianca Jamotte LeRoux, Writer*

"Ma. Ma. Ma. Mama, mama, mama, mama, mama."
"Yes, mama, that's me! I'm your mama."

That single word, repeated over and over, was every dream I ever had of having a daughter coming true before my eyes. From that moment on, every word she learned would be one step closer to all the mother and daughter talks about love, life, the stars, sports, hair, clothes, tea, and everything else that we would have.

I had given birth to my best friend. I talked to her and sung to her every day, and now, well… soon, she was finally going to be able to talk back. My heart grew with each repetition of that beautiful word: mama. She knew me, she loved me, and she knew I was hers.

Her mama.

Our conversations built slowly. At first, we talked about simple things we saw around the neighborhood. My sweet girl would point, name what she saw, and squeal with delight when I understood her. She loved our new way of communicating as much as I did. I loved her funny ways of pronouncing words; blueberries were "booberies," frogs were "fwaggies," and my favorite was at Halloween when she would point out every "bitch" that adorned houses on our block. She had just begun, but she loved to talk and was learning quickly.

Lily was speaking in full sentences by the time she was fifteen months old. By the time she was two, anyone who met her would tell you that every new word or phrase she learned came with more wit and appropriately-used sarcasm than is typical for a child her age. Our conversations quickly turned from:

"I love you to the moon and back, my love."

"I love YOU to the moon and back, my mama!"

To:

"Mama! I don't like chicken! I don't like broccoli! I don't like tomatoes! I have to pee! And I want to watch Peppa Pig!"

"Ok. Can you ask me nicely, please?"

"May I please pee?"

My sweet, chubby-cheeked tot was replaced by a cranky teenager stuck in a toddler's body. She still had those adorable lispy "S's," rounded "R's," and W-sounding "L's," but they were tainted with some serious 'tude. With her desire to speak came her desire to be understood and when she wasn't, I was the problem.

"Where are my chuzes?" Lily asked as she searched under the sofa cushions.

Chuzes? I took a guess - "Your shoes?" I asked as I walked to the entryway closet where she tossed her shoes after playing outside each day. My girl looked up at me like I could not have been more disappointing to her.

"No! My chuuuuuzes. Ugh!" she enunciated, adding the "ugh" for extra emphasis. I was the idiot for not understanding her.

"Your juice?" I suggested, keeping my voice upbeat. Nope. Wrong again.

"No, mama! I said my CHUZES!"

At this point, I was out of ideas, so I threw out "Your Jews?" just for fun.

"Ugh! Never mind! I find it!" She was not having any of my playing around and stomped off. To this day I still have no idea what "chuzes" are.

I got used to my child's way with words and worldly observations. I always spoke to her like a normal person and explained things age-appropriately yet honestly. The few times I spoke baby talk to her she asked me if there was something wrong with my mouth.

As she was approaching four and started "big kid" school, she came home with many "big kid" questions about life and the world.

"Why don't any of the characters on TV have mommas?"
"What does kill mean?"
"What happens when someone dies?"

Oof…I could have used a few more years for some of these questions, but my still very young girl wanted answers. I did my best and used each opportunity to help her learn a bit more about these topics without terrifying her. I found that at this stage, admitting that I don't know or have all the answers about life was sometimes enough for her. I told her that kill means that something or someone makes it so that someone or something doesn't live anymore (no need for more detail there) I explained that this was usually what happened to the mommas in the Disney movies she watched, but it's part of the "backstory," and they don't show it in the movie because that would be too sad. I admitted that I have no idea what happens when we die. Nobody does, really, but there are many different ideas and beliefs, and we get to choose which one we want to believe in.

I hadn't damaged her for life with my answers. I survived this round of questioning and began preparing myself for more to come.

One gorgeous afternoon, she and I sat sunning ourselves through the window at my mom's house. We listened to all the sounds that accompany spring and talked about each as we noticed them; the wind blowing gently through the large leaves on the loquat tree, dogs down the hill playing outside, bees buzzing around the lavender plants just outside the window, a fly bouncing on the window screen in front of us.

Lily was worried about the fly trapped inside the house, so I opened the door a few feet away and told her it would eventually find its way out. As I walked back over to her by the window, I saw she was staring down.

"What did you find, chick?"

She glared at the windowsill, focused. "A fly. What's it doing?"

The fly lay there, lifeless.

My girl looked up at me with her ocean blue eyes and asked, "Is it sleeping?"

She had asked about death each time we watched a Disney movie. Someone always dies in a Disney movie, but this was to be her first time dealing with it in real life. She had no attachments to this fly, but I wanted to tread lightly.

"Remember in the Lion King how Simba's papa falls, and his soul can no longer use his body, so his soul goes back to its spirit self, and his body goes into the ground?"

Lily looked at me in disgust for belittling her intelligence. "It's dead!"

"Yes."

And then she asked every toddler's favorite question. "Why?"

"I don't know, baby. Maybe he got stuck in the window."

And again, "Why?"

"Well, he could have flown too high and—"

"He died because he didn't listen to his momma!"

She said this so matter-of-factly, it stopped my thoughts, and my mind went blank. Before I knew what was happening, I heard myself say, "Yup, that's exactly right."

I have no idea where Lily got the idea that not listening to me could have such severe consequences, but I confirmed the idea that not listening to your mother could result in death. I was horrified with myself for about five seconds… and then declared it a parenting win.

My darling girl is now six and has become more of a kid with only a few teenager-like outbursts here and there. Our relationship is changing as she grows; with communication comes disagreements, and big blow-out fights occasionally. I worry that someday she'll stop talking to me altogether if I don't get things "right" while she is still young. I've already felt her pull away a bit since she started kindergarten. She has her own life now and doesn't always want to share it with me, and I am no longer the only person she turns to for answers to her questions.

Her new favorite way of communicating with me is by leaving notes. She has learned how to state her thesis and defend it, so I have received many letters telling me that ice cream is an excellent choice for dinner with three compelling reasons why, and concluded with "And that is why ice cream is a healthy choice for dinner." With clever attempts at changing the dinner menu, I have also received love notes. I find them taped to the fridge, placed on my pillow/leaned on my face for me to find when I wake up in the morning. Reading the words "To Mama, I love you" for the first time hit me as hard as hearing her first "mama." It reminded me that no matter how our relationship changes, even if she does eventually stop talking to me she knows me, she loves me, I am hers, and she is mine.

FROM WALLFLOWER TO FOUNDING MEMBER OF THE MALL RUNNING CLUB

BRIANNA BELL

> *"Toddlers are seriously self-centered, alarmingly loud, incredibly messy, obnoxiously time-consuming, and they can't even wipe their own butts... but they are cute."* ~ Brianna Bell Writes

Nothing in my life could have prepared me for motherhood, but my pre-baby life was especially poor preparation.

I entered this world a wallflower, floating through my childhood feeling like I was on the outside, not quite comfortable enough to settle in.

But despite being an introverted kid, and an only child, I had this strange obsession with big families. I enjoyed my outsider status and used books to gain access to big families. I adored the Weasley family from Harry Potter, the Pike kids from The Babysitter's Club, and the five sisters from All-of-a-Kind Family.

It was through my 'books with big families' obsession that I decided I would one day have a big family. I never thought about the fact that I craved being alone, and loved quiet and contemplation. I was a wallflower with a purpose, and I clung to the hope of one day creating my own idyllic family. It wasn't until I met my husband and his own book-worthy family, that I finally found my place, and settled in among the flowers.

By twenty-two, I was a mother to the most beautiful daughter, Penelope Rose. She was also the first baby I ever held. Being an outsider in life meant that this was my first introduction to babydom, and it was a crash course beyond anything I ever imagined. The nurses didn't want to let my husband, and I leave the hospital, we were *those* new parents.

Eventually, we were released from the hospital, and I began the life I had always dreamed of. Gone were the days of actually dreaming, because I didn't sleep. Also gone were the days of being a wallflower, because I had no time to cling to any wall. I was covered in the mire of motherhood, and there was no getting out of it now.

I eventually gained my confidence as a mother and even had a second child, and then a third. I was building up my own dream big family, just like the Old Woman in the Shoe. My house wasn't a shoe, although sometimes it felt as small as one. My house was like a Fisher Price museum, all of the primary colors were represented in my living room, thanks to my Exersaucer, baby swing, infant instruments, Jumperoo, and (dumped out) basket full of toys. I was surrounded by the tiny people that I had created, and all their things too.

My children are all curious and adventurous, and I haven't noticed a speck of wallflower-ness within any of them. They're little tornadoes of chaos, and at the center of the storm is my oldest daughter, Penny, my wild child.

As hectic as my life is, I feel like I have finally arrived, and found the place that I belong. It doesn't matter that breast milk is constantly leaking out of my boobs, or that I'm walking around in a sleep-deprived fog, I'm finally living my life, instead of peeping into others.

Now that my kids are getting older I am starting to look back on their younger days with a dash of idealism, picking out the pieces that are most cherished and discarding the rest.

Recently I recalled a day at the mall that took an interesting turn, when I only had two children, and still left the house to go to the mall on my own.

That particular morning I packed my behemoth diaper bag and caught a bus to browse books at the mall. Mothers who take their children shopping are saints, in my eyes, because what child wants to walk through a place full of things they desperately want but cannot have? It's a nightmare for everyone involved, but for some reason, I just really wanted to walk around and look at some books, because old habits die hard, and I was still reading about big families for fun.

The bus pulled up to the curb, and I jolted forward, cheerios spilling all over the floor. Naturally, my three-year-old, Penny, stepped on every cheerio, because she thought it would be funny. I rushed out of the bus and didn't look back, pulling my two kids along with me.

I ended up spending five seconds looking at adult books until Penny ventured over to the Children's area, which was surprisingly not well stocked with literature, but had every toy imaginable.

We played for a while, and then I convinced Penny to stop and grab lunch at the food court. I had my double stroller with me, and my one-year-old, Georgia, was strapped in on one side, but Penny had zero interest in the confines of a stroller.

We walked together to the food court, until suddenly I was walking alone. I looked beside me, where Penny had just been, and saw the back of her as she ran as fast as her tiny legs could go.

"Penny, stop!" I bellowed, in my best angry mom voice.

All eyes were on me now, and then I started to chase after her. She turned left, and I turned left too, pushing my double stroller, my diaper bag bumping me in the knees.

She turned again, and this time three passerby's pointed in the direction she went.

"Thank you," I huffed, and I continued running after her.

After a few twists and turns, I noticed a young teenage girl jogging behind me, and I wondered if she thought I had started a mall running club. She raced past me with her lithe body and shouted back, "I'll grab her."

Never in my wildest dreams did I think a stranger, running through the mall after my child, and shouting those words, would be a balm to my battered soul. But it was.

Something about a strange girl running after her stopped my daughter in her tracks, which come to think of it, is probably not something I should be proud of. I was finally able to catch up with Penny, my face beet red and my heart rate well beyond a healthy cardiovascular level.

"Penelope Rose, do you know how much that scared me?" I shouted, as the helpful teen shrunk back to her mom.

"I don't know? Fifteen?" She replied.

I may have been nearly drunk with exhaustion, raising my armful of babies, but that is a response I will never forget. I laughed, while my three-year-old stared at me wide-eyed, and I pulled her into me and buried my face into her soft curls.

"That's funny, I'm going to put that on Facebook," I said, while strapping her into her stroller, because I'm a Millennial and that is what we do.

In case you're wondering, earlier this year my husband had a vasectomy, after three children I am done, the idealism of massive families snuffed out from the reality of day-to-day childrearing.

Really, I wouldn't trade it for the world. Just don't ask me to take my kids to a mall.

TODDLER BATTLES
LAURA BAUSTIAN

"If I hadn't had boys, I would never have been able to say things like: No, you may not put your crayons in the toaster oven." ~ Adventures by Mom

There are a million and ten things people like to tell new moms and moms-to-be about pregnancy, newborns, and being a mom in general. Some of that advice has value. Some does not. My advice is to do what works for you, your child, and your family. For me and my boys, we came to some agreements early on.

Leaving the house on time was never a challenge for me. I HATE to be late. Then, I had Harley. As a newborn, and an infant, it was easier to get out of the house in a reasonable amount of time. Grab my bags, his bags, pick him up and go. I managed to get places (like work, church, social events) on time probably ninety percent of the time. The other ten percent were due to Harley sleeping past his usual nap time or having huge diaper blowouts right as we were walking out the door. I so looked forward to when he was potty trained. Blowouts would no longer be an issue. Heh. What did I know?

No one told me when you are potty-training a little person, and they say, "I have to go potty." Those words elicit a lightning-fast reflex in a mom. I could have that boy half naked and on the toilet in less than fifteen seconds. I was close to NASCAR fast. Why? Because if you don't make it in time, you are dealing with a crying, wet little one. Changing clothes is like negotiating with a small terrorist. They only want the green dinosaur shirt - NOT the blue one. Well, the green one is wet. And, we don't have time to do laundry right this minute. So, blue dinosaur it is.... Oh my! The tears go from angry to broken hearted. All because mom didn't get the little one to the bathroom quickly enough.

Once the little one has things figured out, you may think you're in the clear. WRONG. Think again. The small terrorist is now an independent, "I do it myself" terrorist. My son is fifteen, and I still have crystal clear memories of the morning he had to use the restroom about ten minutes before we needed to leave. I know, ten minutes, plenty of time - right? Wrong!

I had negotiated somewhat socially acceptable clothing for the day. Meaning everything matched for the most part. There was nothing itchy, scratchy, or too tight. He had put them on, and I thought we were in the clear. I was loading our things into the car when Harley announced, "I go potty now." I told him, "Ok, hurry, we need to leave soon." He assured me he would hurry. This was at 6:50 AM. We needed to leave by 7:00 AM. I could hear him singing and playing. This was definitely not hurrying. I opened the bathroom door.

Harley, startled, yelled, "GET OUT! PRIVACY MOM!!!!" His yelling shocked me, and I shut the door. Then realized I was being bossed around by a three-and-a-half-year-old. I don't think so, buddy. I opened the door again.

Harley had a sheepish grin on his face. All of his clothes were on the floor. Apparently, he needs to be naked to use the restroom.

Exasperated, I said, "If you need to go potty, please go. If not, put your clothes back on so we can leave for school." He said, "Ok. I go potty now," and he hopped on the toilet. I stood and waited. He insisted, "Go 'way mom. Need privacy."

I left the door open but stepped away. He promptly closed the door. Fine. As long as he hurries up I don't care if the door is open or closed. I'm thinking, it's now 7:00 AM. If we do not leave in the next three minutes, at the most, we will miss the magic window of minimal traffic and be late. Then, I heard a clank. A clanking sound is not a normal sound to hear when your son is in the restroom. So, I opened the door - again.

The boy was naked in the bathtub! The clanking was a Hot Wheels Car he had dropped. I had no idea where that came from. Hot Wheels don't belong in the bathroom. He looked up. His eyes got huge. I can only imagine the look that was on my face. Desperately trying to remain calm, and not yell, I took a long, deep breath. Harley realized he was about to go over the line, said, "I sorry Momma. I hurry."

He promptly proceeded to pee in the bathtub. At that point, I was just glad he was done! I washed him off. Grabbed a towel, dried the giggling boy, and wrestled him back into his clothes. We were out the door by 7:10 AM. No, we were NOT on time.

As you may have noticed I negotiated with my toddler regarding his clothes. I purchased clothing that was appropriate, stylish, and what I wanted him to wear. I offered him choices of two outfits. Green and blue shorts with a blue shirt, or grey shorts with a red shirt. He saw this as a pick and choose the menu, kind of like a clothing buffet. He'd pick the green and blue shorts to go with the red shirt, not the intended matching blue shirt. The socks were all white, so they matched everything. I'm thankful for boys because I cannot imagine negotiating with a little girl in terms of clothing, and accessories! My sister has a daughter. I know what a challenge that can be.

One of my favorite outfits for Harley was for Rodeo Day at nursery school. His grandparents bought cute little cowboy Wrangler jeans, a western shirt with pearl snaps, and cowboy boots. He had a cowboy hat, and a belt with a fancy buckle. I had everything washed, ironed and ready to go. No other options were available for negotiation for that day. He reluctantly put it all on as I went on and on about how handsome and what a big boy he would look like. I helped him snap the jeans. He laid down on his bed and held up a socked foot. I wrestled one little foot into the boot, and then the other one.

He tried to stand up. He struggled to roll back and forth, kind of like a turtle on its back. It appeared he couldn't bend at the waist. He finally flopped over onto his stomach, shimmed to the edge of his bed, and let his feet drop to the floor. He managed to stand up, and promptly announced, "These are owie pants. Harwee no wear dem."

No matter how much I tried to negotiate, he was not wearing the Wranglers. He insisted they were too tight and were "owie!" He ended up wearing blue and grey plaid, flannel pajama pants, work boots, and his cute western shirt. At least he wore the shirt. I considered that a partial mom win. I didn't see the point in him having a meltdown over pants that were uncomfortable.

Whether it's over clothes, haircuts, or what to eat remember how little control toddlers really have. Some things are not worth the battle. Choose them wisely. And remember little people, little battles - big people, big battles. So, if you see a mom in the local grocery store, and her little one has on shorts, cowboy boots, a red bandana pirate hat, and an eye patch just smile, nod, and know she wasn't choosing that battle.

IS IT POOP OR IS IT CHOCOLATE?

SHYA GIBBONS

"I know I am not supposed to have favorites, but you are my favorite I whispered to my dog. I hope he doesn't tell the potty-training, sleep-regressing toddler that piece of information."
~Vintage Dreams with a Modern Twist

I have always been a strictly by the book type of person. You should follow the rules. If you want to see results follow XYZ steps to reach your goal, research, prepare, then prepare some more.

When I found out that I was pregnant, I wasted no time buying books that would help me along with my pregnancy and soon to be child. On top of reading the books, I read stories of people's personal accounts. I found lists of things I OMG-absolutely-without-a-doubt needed and bought them, so I was prepared (spoiler alert: I didn't use most of those items.). I had this motherhood thing figured out.

Then I had the baby, and I laughed and laughed and laughed, because that super small, snuggly baby was the one calling the shots. All of my preparations and plans went out the window when the baby came. You know what, though? It was ok. We made it through the first two years with ups and downs, but we made it, and that's what counts.

When it comes to preparing for a toddler? Good luck. That is all I heard: good luck and Godspeed! Are there books? Of course! Do they help? Absolutely not. There is no way to write a book about something that has so many variations. With books about infants it is sleeping, diapers, food, bathing. Toddlers are hope and pray something works out, and invest in a good bathroom cleaner because those little bodies produce a lot of mess. But there are countless things that no books or personal stories will prepare you for, my dear. There are some things you simply must live through- nay, survive through.

No one can prepare you for the moment your heart will grow approximately three million times its size as your little boy whispers, "Momma, you make me so happy. I am so glad that you are my mommy." Of course, while he says this, he will be snuggled in your arms, letting your brain have rapid-fire back flashes of when he was just a little baby. Where have the years gone? You'll wonder why you ever thought the toddler years would be hard because come on, this is adorable!

You will have seconds, minutes, hours, days, maybe even weeks of that attitude if you're lucky. Conversely, you will have days where you hear words coming out of your mouth that you could never have imagined possible.

Just last week with my four-year-old we played the ever exciting, always keeps you on your toes game of 'What Is That?' This round of What Is That was: "Snuggler, um, what is that on your underwear? Is it poop? Is it chocolate? Did you just eat chocolate? Were you just in the bathroom going potty?'

It suddenly becomes an updated, grosser version of the game of Clue. Who did it? Where? With What? Was it the toddler in a corner having an accident? Is it poop? Was it a toddler who refuses to wear pants around the house and he ate chocolate, and it just so happened to get on his underwear?

The Unofficial Guidebook to Surviving Life With Toddlers

We eventually solved our Clue Card: It was the toddler with the chocolate bar in the bathroom.

The how is never quite explained, nor where he had the chocolate hidden away, or the moment he snuck it into the bathroom. Also, jeepers' creepers, don't eat in the bathroom! Especially chocolate!

Find me an instructional book where I can check the appendix for 'is it chocolate or poop on his underwear?' or 'is this pee or juice?' These are tough roads to traverse, but you travel them with those who can help you along the journey. Find your tribe and stick with them because the chances are high of having an unthinkable moment, like the poop or chocolate debacle of '18, and you will need people to laugh with when these things happen.

Mine helped me through potty training, and let me tell you, that was an adventure. I have heard stories; perhaps they are merely parenting urban legends, of children who are potty trained in less than a week. Keeping in line with my beliefs, I went head first into potty training with as much planning and confidence as a general in a war. My son had a special book with his favorite neighborhood tiger on it. The book had a button that made the sound of a flushing potty and included a super cute potty song that my son loved to sing. He picked out his own potty seat with four reptiles on it, and I made a sticker chart. Every time he used the potty he would get a sticker. At the end of one row of stickers, he could get a small present. Once he filled up the entire chart, he would get a trip to the toddler Motherland: Chuck E. Cheese.

I foolishly thought I would have this handled. I did not. He grasped the concept right away but chose not to use the potty. He would sit for fifteen to twenty minutes then get up and pee in his diaper. If he decided to forego the diaper, he would pee on the floor near the bathroom. One time I was on the phone and had to hastily get off of it as I yelled out, "We don't pee on the dog!" Our poor, unsuspecting collie. We went through weeks of zero progress before I called a peace treaty and agreed to try again in a few months. I am proud to say that my now four-year-old is completely potty trained and has moved on to just making it look like he pooped his pants instead of actually pooping them. Little victories, little victories.

That is what it all comes down to with being a parent and raising a little boy: little victories. Not every day is going to be tight hugs around the neck with his sweet, gentle voice whispering how much he loves you. Somedays that little voice will be yelling he wishes Bowser was his father, or that he wants to join the circus until I point out he is afraid of clowns and then he quickly backtracks.

Yet every single night when I tuck him into bed, and he holds my hand and tells me he loves me, all of the craziness of the day fades away. My little boy that, in my mind, was just a tiny baby, is now a big boy who uses the potty, refers to his bath water as tepid on occasion and can hold a conversation about the latest episode of his favorite shows is growing up before my very eyes.

Whenever a friend has a child, I tell them to cherish every second of it, even the bad ones, because there is a heart-wrenching amount of truth behind the saying 'the days are long but the years are short.' I know the upcoming years will have fiascos involving much less disgusting things like poop. They will center around school dances and sports and colleges, and while I help him through those days, I will still look into his soulful blue eyes and remember the small moments of him holding my hand until he falls asleep. Or the extremely rare days he falls asleep snuggled on my lap, and I get to relive his years in the blink of an eye that always ends with a teardrop full of inexplicable love.

PRESCHOOLER MELTDOWNS 101
ASHFORD EVANS

"Some days I really nail this parenting thing. And some days I am certain this three-year-old will be the absolute END of me. #Threenager ~Biscuits and Crazy

Preschool is a special time where your tiny little ball of mush begins to finally develop into a teeny tiny person. You are [hopefully] nearing the end of the full-blown temper tantrums and you can begin to reason and converse with your child. And half the time it seems like they actually understand you!! However, there are a few things that they still just can't even. And most of these will trigger any last remnants of those dreaded nuclear level meltdowns.

1. JUICE BOXES

This deceptive product is marketed directly to your preschooler. It bears the smiling happy faces of their favorite cartoon characters and bright, colorful pictures of fruit ripe at harvest. It comes in a small little package just the right size for sticky little hands to wrap around. But do not be fooled. This is clearly no product for a preschooler.

You see the problem begins with the straw which has been conveniently packaged in its own plastic wrap and glued to the outside of each individual box. Have you ever seen a preschooler try to retrieve said straw from its cozy little plastic cocoon? Think total and utter meltdown. They simply do not have the wherewithal to figure out how to open this neat little package. My kindergartener has figured out where we keep the kitchen scissors and uses these. Which is exactly what I want…my five year old trying to use kitchen scissors to cut open a teeny tiny package. Quite frankly this is how we lose teeny tiny fingers.

So let's say you get past the straw debacle. Now your preschooler must apply the precise amount of pressure to the box to propel the juice into his mouth- but not so much that the juice goes spurting out all over his face, eyes, and the dog. I don't know about your kid, but mine doesn't do things "just a little." We have two levels: Not enough and Old Faithful.

2. TOOTHPASTE

I'm not sure who has designed the toothpaste "snap cap," but I am convinced it will remain sealed and keep that toothpaste fresh through a nuclear holocaust. Half the time even I can't get the damned thing open. I pull, I pry, I use my teeth, but that sucker just won't budge. Forget about my child begin able to manipulate the thing with her chubby stubby fingers. Once Daddy comes in to help us we have the same issue as the juice box. The pressure necessary to squeeze just the right amount of the toothbrush is a skill that must be practiced and honed. "Ahhhhhh Little Grasshopper, not yet. Keep trying." Meanwhile, I'm stuck scraping and scrubbing hot pink toothpaste out of the sink, the counter, the hand towels, the floor, and any other surface she may have come in contact with.

3. JACKETS (AND OMG GLOVES)

Could anything be harder for a preschooler? Not only do you have to get a specific arm into a specific hole. But then you have to do it again! And then there is usually some sort of a zipper or a button or some other closure device that makes the whole thing nearly impossible. Add to this the ticking time clock because "WE HAVE TO BE IN THE CAR IN FIVE MINUTES!" And it's just too much. It's just too much!

Why do gloves even come in a preschool size? Has anyone actually ever successfully gotten gloves onto a child of this age? Despite lacking the mental capacity to understand the instructions of "Spread apart all of your fingers. Now don't move." This is just too much to ask. The concentration required to stay focused on the task at hand just escapes them. I can barely even get mittens on my kid's hands, and that's only the thumb to worry about. Forget about successfully getting all five fingers into their respective finger holes. Geez….we thought the jacket was difficult!!

4. WIPING

So I don't know if it's a universal thing or if it's just my kids. But they are born with these little alligator arms that just don't freaking reach. If they can't touch the top of their own heads, I certainly can't expect them to be able to wipe their own butts! And so we wait for nature to take its course and for their teeny tiny arms to grow to an acceptable length. And we think "At last!!"

But don't go running through the fields of freedom just yet my friend. There is still the issue of "appropriate amount of toilet paper." Now, this is a delicate balance, and it lands somewhere in between "using your bare hand" and "single-handedly destroying the remaining South American rain forest." There is also the issue of "correct pressure" (this seems to be becoming a common theme here) and the dreaded "finger slip" or "breakthrough." Who knew that such a seemingly simple task could have such intricacies?

5. POPSICLES

The first issue to arise is the color. This is enough to send me headfirst into the deep freeze to try to retrieve the last pink Popsicle as if it were the last beer in the cooler at an all-day lake party. Next, they're too cold, and then they're too melty and then they're all over the damn floor, the cabinets, and the walls. Sticky little hands rubbing tearful little eyes leaving the perfect sweet and salty streaks down their chubby little cheeks.

Heaven help us if you happen to throw away the push pop package before your cherub has had a chance to pour the remaining liquid all over the floor while attempting to drink it. Then you will find yourself negotiating with a terrorist who is high on a sugar rush and precariously approaching naptime. I find it's just better to explain that "the store ran out of popsicles."

6. AUTOMATICALLY FLUSHING TOILETS

Let's be honest here…I can barely negotiate an automatically flushing toilet. You lean over just a tad too far and WHOOSH!!! Ice cold public toilet water all up in your nether regions. Nothing. Nothing is more unpleasant. But somehow I expect my Tasmanian devil of a preschooler to sit still long enough to finish his business without setting off the damn motion detector? This is an impossible mission. So I have learned to hover just close enough to be able to scoop him up off the toilet as he screams in terror at the whirlpool below him threatening to suck him down into the pipes never to be seen again. I swear my kids have PTSD from the damn toilets at the mall and they began twitching as soon as we walk into the restroom, and they hear the dreaded "WHOOSH" from some other unfortunate soul.

ABOUT THE AUTHORS

Laura Baustian has two boys and works in an elementary school so she never has a boring day. Reading blogs, looking at Pinterest, and sharing stories with her sister, Julie, and cousin, Natalie, lead her to decide that it would be great fun to start a blog together so that everyone else…or whoever is amused, could laugh with them at all the humor they find in daily life. Because we all know if you don't choose joy and laughter, you'll end up crying. Laura looks for the joy. It may take a glass of wine (or martini) to help her find it, but she knows it's there. Find the joy with her at adventuresbymom.com.

Brianna Bell is a wife to Daniel, and mom to Penelope, Georgie, and Eloise. Brianna has been published in over thirty print and digital publications. When she's not writing, you can find her reading, making granola, eating her granola, or going for a walk with her kids.

Shannon Brescher Shea is a mom of two young boys who's just trying to make a difference. Living in the suburbs of Washington D.C., she writes about her adventures learning to be kinder and more sustainable at We'll Eat You Up, We Love You So. She's also published articles about parenting in the Washington Post, Pregnant Chicken, Her View from Home, Ravishly, and Romper. In her day job, she is a senior science writer/editor for the federal government.

Lyndee Brown is Haden and Ryland's mom. She has been married to her husband Matt for ten years. She has a bachelor's of science degree and works as a Respiratory Therapist during the day. At night she moonlights as Superwoman. She is very fluent in sarcasm and can burn toast with the best of them. She is the co-founder of the blog hashtagllifewithboys.com.

Shannon Carpenter is a humorist that lives in Kansas City, Mo where his three children keep him constantly entertained. He enjoys long walks with his dog and explaining to his wife that he is done having any new children. Represented by Chris Kepner.

Lauren Eberspacher is the author and speaker of the blog From Blacktop to Dirt Road where she gives heartfelt Biblical encouragement for the everyday mama and wife. She and her husband Eric live on their grain farm in southeast Nebraska with their three small children. Her devotional, *Midnight Lullabies*, is being released in April of 2019.

Ashford Evans is a single-working mom to three kids, three kittens, two tadpoles, one Chihuahua, and one hamster. For real y'all it's like Animal Kingdom over here. She consistently forgets things and is late everywhere she goes- but she loves to laugh and make other people laugh. And that is her saving grace. She blogs about her crazy escapades and living life in between being the bread winner and the bread maker at biscuitsandcrazy.net. Most recently she became known as "the urinal cake lady" (for real ya'll google it). She has been featured in US Weekly, Independent Review Journal, Pop Sugar, Mom Babble, Scary Mommy, and the Huffington Post.

Shya Gibbons is founder of Vintage Dreams with a Modern Twist and a contributor to the books; I Just Want to Be Perfect and You Do You. Her work has appeared on Sammiches & Psych Meds, McSweeney's Internet Tendency, and The Mighty. She is happily married to an incredible man who doubles as her best friend. They have a five-year-old little boy who lights up their life. Check out her work at www.facebook.com/VintageDreamsWithAModernTwist.

Karsson Hevia is an Author (The Unofficial Guide to Surviving Life with Boys, The Unofficial Guidebook to Surviving Pregnancy without losing your mind), Mother of three, and a Content Writer, Blogger, and Social Media Strategist working in the Bay Area (while maintaining her deep Midwest roots). Karsson writes about the excruciatingly beautiful juxtaposition of motherhood and her continual desire to find the so-called balance of life on her Blog: 2ManyOpenTabs.

Cassie Hilt is a mother to three tiny humans, and the creator of the blog: The Chronicles of Motherhood. She works on maintaining the delicate balance of work/mommy/wife life, and making sure she doesn't run out of wine before payday. She enjoys writing about the authentic moments of parenting---the good, the bad, and the gross. She has contributed to sites such as The Huffington Post, Scary Mommy, and Love What Matters. You can follow her on Facebook at The Chronicles of Motherhood, or visit her website at www.cassiehilt.com.

Sarah Honey is the author of a popular lifestyle blog, "Thank You Honey" where she writes about her every day. Her work has appeared on Mamalode, Scary Mommy, Erma Bombeck, Great Moments in Parenting, 6 ABC Philadelphia and Huffington Post. You can also find her on Twitter, Facebook, Instagram, & Pinterest or wrangling her son.

Adrienn Hunt is a freelance editor and published author living in Southern Michigan with her husband and two daughters. After stay-at-home-momming the crap out of her kids she re-entered civilization as an early literacy advocate and children's librarian. Her irreverent voice has been featured on Blog Her, Bloggy Moms, Parent Society and irregularly published on her blog, adriennhunt.com.

Bianca Jamotte LeRoux is a mom, award-winning filmmaker, actress, writer, and creator of the series Real Mommy Confessions. Her acting career began in musical theater and quickly turned to commercials, print, and TV. Bianca's most exciting role to date is undoubtedly her job as a mom, which brings on a daily host of challenges and accomplishments, often simultaneously. These include successfully keeping her 6-year old from nose diving off the sofa, as well as negotiating with her willful 7-year old. Shortly after the birth of her second child, feeling isolated in the 'burbs she created the web series Real Mommy Confessions, real confessions from real moms all over the world. What started as a project to create community and find the comedy in the chaos of parenthood, turned into two seasons of an award-winning series. Bianca is thrilled to be a part of the "Unofficial Guide" crew. Thank you, Tiffany and Lyndee.

Diana Kane is a wife, mom, and frequent companion to coffee and chaos. She is a proud supporter of ice cream cake for breakfast and perpetually struggles with being on time. Diana spends her days chasing her tail in a kindergarten classroom and her evenings as an unpaid Uber driver to her children's sporting events. She recently published her first book, "Mama Needs A Cupcake," chronicling the chaotic woes of motherhood.

Andrew Knott is a writer from Orlando, Florida and father of three. He has contributed writing to the Washington Post, McSweeney's Internet Tendency, Scary Mommy, Fatherly, The Funny Times, and Weekly Humorist, among others. He is also the author of Fatherhood: Dispatches from the Early Years, a book of essays and stories. For more, visit his website, www.ExplorationsOfAmbiguity.com.

Karen Lesh is a tap-dancing, poetry-writing, chocolate-loving, fulltime working mom of THREE BOYS (who are pure rascal with a side of sweetness). When she's not cleaning a toilet (3 boys!!!), breaking up a wrestling match, enjoying family time, or working her corporate job as a Marketing executive, she blogs about parenting and the adventures of being a Mother of Boys (M.O.B.) at M.O.B. Truths (www.mobtruths.com). Her work has been published on Scary Mommy, Her View from Home, Today Parents, and more. Karen is excited to build a community of moms as she shares her humorous and really real look on the daily life of a parent, through parenting tips/tricks, relatable stories and lots of laughs on the blog and social media.

Jennifer Lizza is a wife, mom, writer, runner, sleep enthusiast, and blogger at Outsmarted Mommy. Her two boys outsmart her daily, although in her defense it could be the lack of sleep. When she's not cracking people up on Twitter she can be found making them cry with her sentimental writing online in The Huffington Post, Scary Mommy, TODAY Parents, and What The Flicka?. Her kids are not the least bit impressed; they just want to know what's for dinner. Jennifer and her firefighting husband call New

Jersey home and when she is not writing, running or daydreaming about a nap you can often find her out with her family eating pizza and ice cream.

Joe Medler is the author of 'Notes from a Developing Dad' and the writer of the Developing Dad blog. He lives in New Jersey with his wife, who is far too good for him, and his two sons, who are both his pride and joy as well as entirely too tall for their ages.

Tiffany O'Connor is the originator, author, and co-editor of *The Unofficial Guidebook to Surviving* series. She is the writer behind the popular blog #lifewithboys. Her work appears in several anthologies, including *Chicken Soup for the Soul My (Kind of) America*. Tiffany is a mom to two amazing, energetic, and fearless human boys and two loveable furry boy dogs. She is married to her high school sweetheart and has three college degrees. Her hobbies include watching television shows about zombies, hiding in her hot tub with a glass of champagne, and listening to Taylor Swift songs on repeat.

Stephanie Ortiz is a married SAHM of 6 who still can't quite figure out how she deviated from her original life plan of traveling the globe as a single, mad professor with too many cats & no kids. She enjoys blogging in her spare time, because it's cheaper than therapy. She's a staff writer for Filter Free Parents, & her work has been featured in *The Huffington Post*, *The Daily Mail*, *Reader's Digest*, & *The Steve Harvey Show*. She may maintain the facade of a mature, suburban housewife, but she's really an overgrown teenager that still enjoys pranking friends & air-guitaring to Nine Inch Nails. Find her at her blog, Six Pack Mom.

Jackie Pick is a former teacher and current writer living in the Chicago area. She is a contributing author to several anthologies, including Multiples Illuminated, Nevertheless We Persisted, and So Glad They Told Me: Women Get Real about Motherhood, Here in the Middle, as well as the literary magazines The Sun and Selfish. Her essays have won awards and commendations from the Royal Nonesuch Humor Writing Competition sponsored by the Mark Twain House and Museum and the WOW! Women on Writing Nonfiction Essay Contest. Jackie is a contributor at Humor Outcasts, and her work has been featured on various online sites including Mamalode, The Her Stories Project, and Scary Mommy. A graduate of the University of Chicago and Northwestern University, Jackie is co-creator and co-writer of the award-winning short film Fixed Up, and a proud member of the 2017 Chicago cast of Listen to Your Mother.

Renee Robbins is a Midwestern-based writer, mother, and part-time curmudgeon. She's been published in Cosmopolitan, Marie Claire, The Elephant Journal and others. She lives in Kansas with her husband, two children and six cats and is NOT writing a book. But she thinks about it a lot.

K.C. Runkel is a former marketer turned stay-at-home mom. She has been published in the anthologies Emerging Writers: An Anthology of Fiction and America's Emerging Writers, as well as Chicken Soup for the Soul: Messages from Heaven and Other Miracles. She is also a contributing writer for Her View from Home. You can follow her blog, The Rustic Hideaway, or her writing page, K.C. Runkel.

Jesica Ryzynski is a writer and mom to four children ranging in age from kindergarten to high school. She writes honestly about the challenges of raising children of all age groups at the same time, mental illness in children and teens and the importance of coffee and humor while navigating it all. Her absolute goal as a writer is to bring back the village by writing honestly about the challenges of parenting and encouraging others to share without fear of judgement. Her work can be found on That's Inappropriate, Savvy Mom, YMC, Motherly and Sammiches and Psych Meds and Her View from Home.

Holly Rust is a native Texan but currently resides in the great city of Chicago with her husband and two sons. She spent over ten years as a corporate executive in the luxury hotel industry. She is now a writer, author and business owner. She is the creator and voice behind Hollydays Chicago, a lifestyle blog where she shares family travel adventures and her favorite food, fashion, and beauty finds. Her essays can be found in several anthologies available on Amazon. You can also find her work on Huffpost, Scary Mommy, Town and Country, Good Housekeeping, TODAY Parenting Team, Yahoo, MSN, and many more.

Sandra Samoska has a background in communication and journalism, and spent the first part of her career writing for various newspapers in Texas and Missouri. She's a freelance writer and a work from home mom of four amazing kids – three girls and one young boy. Sandra's writing has been featured on Her View from Home, Today Parents, Scary Mommy and in the Focus on the Family Magazine. When she's not being a teacher, chauffeur, housekeeper, mentor, psychologist, logistical coordinator, referee and everything else that goes into motherhood, you can find her writing on her blog, Outnumbered, at www.sandrasamoska.com. She lives in Texas with her husband, four kids, two dogs, two gerbils and a turtle.

Michelle Tan is the absurdist comic writer and certified life nonsense expert behind "Ms Awesome, Mother Extraordinaire" (@msawesomemother), the Facebook Page about surviving parenting. She married her husband because he understands her jokes, has three lovely children, two of whom are now teenagers and have veto powers over her writings and Fin, the best black lab dog, who is more famous on Instagram (@finiantheblacklab) than anyone else in the family. She works full time and sleeps part time, and wishes that she could just eat chocolate all day.

Rita Templeton is a mom trying to retain at least a shred of her pre-mom coolness while raising her four sons (yes, four. Yes, all boys. No, she isn't trying for a girl). The struggle is real, and she has chronicled hers on her personal blog, Fighting Off Frumpy, along with major media outlets such as Scary Mommy (where she now works as Associate Editor), PopSugar, and HuffPost. Follow her on Facebook, Instagram, and Twitter @fightingfrumpy ... just don't send her any hate mail.

Carrie Tinsley is a mom of three, a wife, a writer, and kind of a mess if we're being honest. She recently returned to work after being a stay-at-home mom and loves to tell her bad parenting stories so people feel better about their life choices. She reads constantly, enjoys a good beer, and writes sometimes sweet / sometimes sassy posts at Carrie on Y'all (www.carrieonyall.com). She recently appeared in print in The Unofficial Guide to Surviving Life with Boys. You can follow her on Facebook, Twitter, or Instagram.

Briton Underwood is a published Writer, proud father of three, and occasionally a really rad dude. His work can be found on Scary Mommy, Mamalode, THE UNOFFICIAL GUIDEBOOK TO SURVIVING series, and Multiples Illuminated. Published both online and in print.

Amy Weatherly loves red lipstick, graphic tees, and Diet Dr. Pepper a little more than she thinks that she probably should. Most days you can find her lounging in sweatpants and running kids from one place to the other like a crazy person. Her family is her home and her passion is helping women find courage, confidence, and the deep-rooted knowledge that their life has a deep and significant purpose. You can follow her journey at Amyweatherly.com and on Facebook and Instagram.

Sherry White writes about the messiness of life, parenting, and faith at her blog The Messy Christian. She tries to add her own brand of humor and insight into everyday issues we all face, reminding us that even though we find ourselves in countless messes, God's grace lights the way.

LETTER FROM THE EDITORS

Thank you for reading this book. We hope you loved it. We were so lucky to have a fantastic squad of outstanding writers agree to join us on this journey. I hope they all know how much we appreciate each and every one of them. If you enjoyed their stories in this book make sure you check out their blogs, Facebook pages, Twitter feeds, and fabulous Instagram posts.

The toddler years are amazing, frustrating, hilarious, challenging, exciting, and they go by far too quickly. Before you know it your little one will go from fearless toddler to independent teenager. You will look fondly back at the years of building blanket forts and fighting with your child over the color of their plate when you are giving them driving lessons and arguing with them over their curfew. Enjoy every silly mispronounced word and sloppy kiss during toddlerhood and know during the hardest times with your little person that this too shall pass.

This book was created with the goal of showing what it is really like raising toddlers. As you can tell from our stories, every child is unique and special in his or her own way, and every parent is just trying to do their best. If you feel like it is tough and if you are afraid that you are not doing it correctly… you are not alone. We all feel that way sometimes. Just take a deep breath and know that you are doing a good job (I know that because you care enough to read parenting books like this one)

If you found this book to be hilarious, heartwarming, and relatable, we would love it if you told your friends about it and we would be extremely grateful if you would take the time to write a review on Amazon. If you are raising boys check out our book, The Unofficial Guide to Surviving Life with Boys and if you are pregnant or need to get a baby shower gift for a pregnant friend check out our book, The Unofficial Guide to Surviving Pregnancy.

XOXO,
Tiffany & Lyndee

www.ingramcontent.com/pod-product-compliance
Lightning Source LLC
LaVergne TN
LVHW092324080426
835508LV00039B/525